SPEAK CHINESE TODAY

SPEAK CHINESE TODAY

A Basic Course
in the
Modern Language

BEVERLY HONG

with the assistance of
Zhu Bingyao

CHARLES E. TUTTLE COMPANY
Rutland, Vermont & Tokyo, Japan

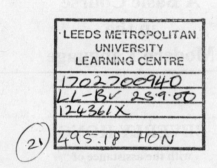
Published by the Charles E. Tuttle Company, Inc.
of Rutland, Vermont & Tokyo, Japan
with editorial offices at
2-6 Suido 1-chome, Bunkyo-ku, Tokyo 112

© 1991 by Charles E. Tuttle Publishing Co., Inc., based on material
first published as *Situational Chinese* by the New World Press, Beijing

LCC Card Number 91-65063
ISBN 0-8048-1701-4 (Book & cassette)
ISBN 0-8048-1715-4 (Book only)

First edition, 1991
Third printing, 1993

Printed in Japan

For John
and
Leta and Hanson
*who use the language
in yet other situations*

CONTENTS

PART TWO

ACKNOWLEDGMENTS

In the course of compiling this material, I have had the assistance of many individuals, both in the People's Republic of China, during many visits there, and among exchange visitors from the People's Republic resident overseas. Linguists, anthropologists and sociologists would conventionally call these people "informants," but researchers whose findings are based on field work would agree that the worth of their work has first to be judged on the accuracy of the data, here defined as "sayability," in today's society. I thus think of my informants as collaborators and I have chosen to name Zhu Bingyao as foremost among all those who have helped me with various portions of this text. Others include members of the staff of the Beijing Language Institute, including Zhu, where I held a week-long session in August 1978. In addition, An Hongzhi and Chen Zhaoguo of the Mathematics Institute and Li Peng of the Microbiology Institute of the Chinese Science Academy, and Ma Binghua of the Guangzhou Foreign Language Institute have been kind enough to read and make some changes in usage in the text.

Mr. Peter Lee and Mrs. Lin of the Hong Kong University Language Centre have also made extensive comments. The latter's comment "It makes me homesick" reassured me about the language not losing its touch with the society from which Mr. Lee and Mrs. Lin recently migrated to Hong Kong. Colleagues and students of ANU have also contributed comments, among them Geremie Barme, Julie Beattie, Anita Chang, and Celia Gerovich.

Leslie Chan, Doris Corson, Jane Lock, Ni Huaying, Ching Pingtang and Kerrie Tarrant have helped me with many of the drafts.

Jon Whalan, having had the experience of intensive language training in the U.S. (Monterey Language School and Georgetown University) and of the intensive language course at Shanghai East China University, was able to help me with his insights from experience in programs in both countries.

I am indebted to Chao Yuan Ren for the concept of sayable Chinese — not only the theory but the practice I gained by translating his sayable English *Grammar of Spoken Chinese* into sayable Chinese. He also did me the kindness of reading and commenting on my texts.

My gratitude to Liu Ts'un is twofold: firstly, for making detailed comments based on his erudition. Many colleagues in Australia and overseas have benefited from him in this way and I am happy to be included in the growing list of benefactees. Secondly, he provided the administrative flexibility that made the development of an innovative text possible.

Li Fang Kuei, the great American Indianist and Sino-Tibetanist, has taught me in his quiet and contemplative manner that the language classroom is a place for field work on language contact and contrast.

Finally, members of my family have given me constant support at home and during many field trips. This book is dedicated to them.

INTRODUCTION

How to Use This Book

Speak Chinese Today is a complete, ungraded course in the Beijing dialect of modern spoken Chinese. Sometimes referred to as Mandarin in the West, this dialect is the official language of the People's Republic of China (where it is called *putonghua*) and Taiwan (where it is called *guoyu*). Twenty-five dialogues, rendered in *pinyin* (the official romanized orthography of China), Chinese characters, and English translation, comprise the core of the course.

The text was designed especially so that it could be used by those studying Chinese on their own as well as in the classroom, and by beginning students as well as intermediate speakers of the language. Supplemental support material for self-study and beginning students includes vocabulary lists, grammar notes, and pronunciation exercises.

For those who have studied Chinese, the lessons provide practice using familiar vocabulary in a variety of situations. These students will likely skip the pronunciation practice and begin directly with the dialogues. It is recommended that students listen to the dialogues first for overall comprehension, then several more times for details, before seeking recourse to the vocabulary lists and notes provided.

Beginning students should work with the pronunciation exercises (the first portion of the tape; transcribed beginning on text p. 217) until they feel quite familiar with the *pinyin* orthography and have no trouble producing and comprehending the four tones. Although tapes are an excellent resource for both aural and oral practice, the assistance of a native speaker of the language, particularly in the beginning stages, is also highly desirable.

CHINESE PHONETICS

A Chinese syllable is divided into two parts, the *sheng,* or "initial," and the *yun,* or "final." For example, the word *ding,* referring to a type of ancient Chinese bronze, is composed of the initial sound *d,* and the final sound *ing. Ding* is pronounced as in the English "ding dong."

INITIALS

There are twenty-three initial sounds in Chinese. As in the word *ding,* above, many of these sounds have fairly approximate English equivalents. Of the initials, these include:

b	as in "bear"	*p*	as in "pearl"
d	as in "dirt"	*t*	as in "time"
g	as in "girl," always hard	*k*	as in "key"

Some initials form pairs of "aspirated" and "unaspirated" sounds. When pronounced, the aspirated sounds, *b, d,* and *g,* are accompanied by a strong puff of air. A piece of paper placed an inch or so from the lips should move when these sounds are pronounced. The unaspirated sounds, *p, d,* and *k,* are pronounced with no accompanying puff of air. A piece of paper in front of the lips should not move when they are pronounced.

There are also sounds that have no close English equivalents and these, naturally, cause the most trouble for native-English speakers. Of the initials these include:

z   as the "ds" in "cards," but pronounced with the tip of the tongue closer to the teeth *c*   as the "ts" in "its," but pronounced with the tip of the tongue closer to the teeth

zh   as the "dge" in "judge," but pronounced with the tongue drawn further back and pressed against the roof of the mouth

ch   as the "ch" in "cheese," but pronounced with the tip of the tongue drawn more toward the back of the mouth

j   as in "jet," but with the tongue drawn further back and with some space between it and the roof of the mouth

q   as the "ch" in "choo-choo" (train), but with the tongue drawn further back and with some space between it and the roof of the mouth

Note that *c, ch*, and *q* are the aspirated counterparts of *z, zh*, and *j*. Other initials that differ from their English counterparts are:

s   as in "sir," but with the tip of the tongue more to the front of the mouth

sh   as in "shirt," but with the tongue pulled to the back of the mouth

x   as the hissing sound when "s" and "y" in "bless you" are run together; it is somewhere between "s" and "sh"

h   as the "ch" in the German *ach*

r   as in "run," but with the tip of the tongue drawn well to the back of the mouth and without pursing the lips

FINALS

There are twenty-nine finals in standard Chinese. Again, many have close English equivalents:

a   as in "father" or "ah"

o   as in "or"

u   as the "oo" in "ooze"

ü   as its German counterpart (but written *yu* when it appears with no initial)

Some finals are pronounced differently depending upon the initials, if any, they appear in combination with. For example:

i   as in "ski"; this final sometimes appears with no initial, when it is written as *yi*

i   as the "ou" in "could" following *s, c,* or *z*

i   as the "er" in "her" following *r, zh, ch,* or *sh,* but with the tip of the tongue pulled back and placed closer to the roof of the mouth

The *e* final also has several variants:

e as in "herb" when it follows initials *d, t, n, l, g, k, h, z, c, s, zh, ch, r*

e as in the unstressed English article "a," when it appears in a syllable of neutral tone

e as in "yes," when following *y, ü,* or, sometimes, when standing alone; to avoid confusion, this sound is sometimes romanized as *ê*

FINALS IN COMBINATION

When two or more finals are combined, each letter retains its original sound value, although the following combinations undergo slight modifications:

ai   as in "aisle"

ei   as in "eight"

ian as the "ien" in "Vienna"

ie   as the "ye" in "yes"

uai as rhyming with "why"

uan as in "iguana"; however, when following *j, q, x,* and *y,* the *u* is in fact *ü* and *uan* sounds more like *uen*

ue   as in "duet"

ui   as rhyming with "way"

There are four basic tones in standard spoken Chinese, commonly referred to as the first, second, third, and fourth tones. The word *ma*, for example, can be pronounced in four different ways, and each has a distinct meaning. When romanized, these are usually indicated by diacritical marks (as they are in the text), as follows: *mā*, meaning "mother"; *má*, meaning "hemp"; *mǎ*, meaning "horse"; and "*mà*," meaning "to scold."

The first tone is a level tone; it starts and finishes at the same high pitch. The second tone is a rising tone; it starts from a middle pitch and rises to a high pitch. The third tone starts from a low-middle pitch, drops to low, then rises to high-middle pitch. The fourth tone is a falling tone; it starts from a high pitch and falls to a low pitch.

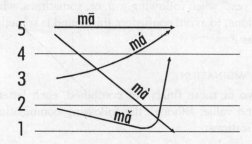

PITCH LEVEL OF THE FOUR TONES

There is also a so-called "neutral tone," indicated by the absence of a diacritical mark over the syllable. Such syllables are pronounced short and soft, and vary in pitch depending upon which tone they follow: after first and second tones they are pronounced at middle pitch; after third tone they are pronounced at middle-high pitch; and after fourth tone, they are pronounced at low pitch.

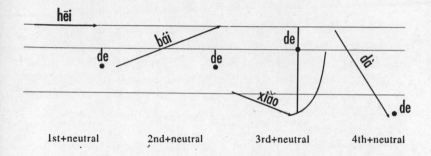

| 1st+neutral | 2nd+neutral | 3rd+neutral | 4th+neutral |

Note that, even though different people speak with different pitch ranges, the relative tone contours remain the same.

Obviously, pronunciation of a tone may change slightly depending upon the tone that precedes or follows it. However, the third tone changes in a pronounced manner: when followed by a first, second, fourth, or neutral tone, it loses its final rise (only the initial portion remains), and when followed by another third tone, it changes to a second tone.

PART ONE

DÌ YĪ KÈ

CHĪGUO FÀN LE MA?

Jiǎ: Xiǎolǐ, chīguo fàn le ma?

Yǐ: Chīguo le. Xiànzài dōu jiǔdiǎn zhōng le.
Zěnme, nǐ hái méi chī a?

Jiǎ: Zuótian wǎnshang shuìde wǎn, jīntian zǎoshang jiù qǐlai wǎn le, shítáng yǐjing guān mén le.

Yǐ: Ng, dào xiǎochībù qù kànkan yǒu shénme chī de.

Jiǎ: Duì, wǒ zhè jiù qù.

Yǐ: Zǒu, wǒ gēn nǐ yíkuàr qù. Hái yǒu jǐ fēn zhōng cái shàngkè ne.

Jiǎ: Nà hǎojíle. Zǒu ba.

Yǐ: Yàoshi xiǎochībù bù kāimén, nǐ kě yào è dùzi le.

Jiǎ: Shǎo chī yí dùn yě wúsuǒwèi.

LESSON 1

HAVE YOU EATEN?

A: Xiaoli, have you eaten yet?

B: Yes, I've eaten. It's already nine. Why, haven't you eaten yet?

A: I went to bed late last night, so I got up late this morning. The dining hall is already closed.

B: Hm, go to the snack bar and see if there's anything to eat.

A: Right, I'll go now.

B: Come on, I'll go with you. There are still a few minutes before class time.

A: That's great. Let's go.

B: If the snack bar isn't open you'll surely go hungry.

A: Skipping a meal doesn't bother me.

第一课　吃过饭了吗？

甲：小李，吃过*[1]饭了[2]吗[3]？

乙：吃过了。现在都[4]九点钟了，怎么，你还没[5]吃啊[6]？

甲：昨天晚上睡得[7]晚，今天早上就起来晚[8]了，食堂已经关门了。

乙：嗯[9]！到小吃部去[10]看看[11]有什么吃的[12]。

甲：对，我这[13]就[14]去。

乙：走，我跟[15]你一块儿去，还有几分钟才[16]上课呐（呢）[17]！

甲：那好极了，走吧[18]。

乙：要是小吃部不开门，你可[19]要[20]饿肚子[21]了。

甲：少吃一顿也[22]无所谓。

---

*See Grammar and Usage, p. 150.

LESSON 1: VOCABULARY

第	dì-	prefix for ordinal numbers
一	yī	one
课（課*）	kè	lesson, class
吃	chī	to eat
过（過）	-guo	aspect marker for indefinite past; to have had the experience of
饭（飯）	fàn	meal, rice (cooked)
了	le	modal particle to show change of state, noting new situation
吗（嗎）	ma	interrogative particle
现在（現～）	xiànzài	now
都	dōu	all, already
九	jiǔ	nine
点钟（點鐘）	diǎn (-zhōng)	o'clock
怎么（～麼）	zěnme	how, why
你	nǐ	you (singular)
还（還）	hái	still, yet
没有	méi (-you)	have not
昨天	zuótian	yesterday
晚上	wǎnshang	night, evening, during night-time, in the evening
睡，睡觉（～覺）	shuì, shuì jiào	to sleep, to go to bed
得	de	general particle for complements. Here used as complement of result.
晚	wǎn	late

Characters in parentheses are Complicated forms.

今天	**jīntian**	today
早上	**zǎoshang**	morning, during the morning
就	**jiù**	then, therefore, will immediately
起来（～來）	**qǐlai**	get up
食堂	**shítáng**	dining hall
已经（～經）	**yǐjing**	already
关（關）	**guān**	to shut, to close
门（門）	**mén**	door
嗯	**e, ng,**	acknowledging attention; notice of what the other person is saying.
到…去	**dào . . . qu**	to go to
小吃部	**xiǎochībù**	snack bar
去	**qù**	to go (definite direction)
看	**kàn**	to look, to see, to read, to have a look.
看看	**kàn-kan**	to have a look, all reduplicated forms express tentativeness
有	**yǒu**	to have, there is/are, existence
什么（～麼）	**shénme**	what
的	**de**	norminalizer changing the preceding verb phrase into a noun phrase.
对（對）	**duì**	right, correct
我	**wǒ**	I, me
这＝这会儿（這會兒）	**zhè（＝zhehuěr）**	this, this moment
就	**jiù**	at once, immediately
走	**zǒu**	walk, go
跟	**gēn**	and, with conjoining nouns only (in speech)

一块儿（～塊儿）	**yíkuàr**	together, in one piece
几（幾）	**jǐ**	several; how many
分钟（～鐘）	**fēn (zhōng)**	minutes
才	**cái**	before, only then
上课（～課）	**shàngkè** ＝**shàng＋kè**	to be in class, to have a class either to teach or to attend
呐＝呢	**ne**	particle having same locutional force as "you see"
那，那么（～麼）	**nà, nàme**	in that case
好	**hǎo**	good
极了（極～）	**-jíle**	extremely, a complement
吧	**ba**	particle of supposition, consultation, suggestion, plea or polite command
要是	**yàoshi**	if, in case ... then; shall, will; want to, must
不	**bù**	no, not, negative
开（開）	**kāi**	open
可	**kě**	will surely, emphatic adverb
饿（餓）	**è**	hungry
肚子	**dùzi**	stomach
少	**shǎo**	less, few
顿（頓）	**dùn**	measure word for meals
也	**yě**	also
无所谓（無～謂）	**wúsuǒwèi**	fixed expression from Classical Chinese for "it doesn't matter"

DÌ ÈR KÈ

ZÀI XIǍOCHĪBÙ

Jiǎ: Tóngzhì, yǒu tián miànbāo ma?

Yǐ: Yǒu a. Nǐ yào yíngyǎng miànbāo háishi nǎiyóu miànbāo?

Jiǎ: Yí yàng yíge ba.

Yǐ: Hái yào shénme?

Jiǎ: Zài lái wǎn dòujiāng.

Yǐ: Hái yào bíede ma?

Jiǎ: Bú yào le, yígòng duōshǎo qián?

Yǐ: Liǎng máo.

Jiǎ: (náchu qián lai)

Yǐ: Nǐ zhè shì yíkuàiqián, zhǎo gěi nǐ bāmáo.

LESSON 2

AT THE SNACK BAR

A: Comrade, do you have any sweet rolls?

B: Yes, do you want healthbread or butterbread?

A: Could I have one of each?

B: What else do you want?

A: And a bowl of soybean milk.

B: Anything else?

A: That will be all, how much altogether?

B: Twenty cents.

A: (*takes out money*)

B: Here's eighty cents change for your dollar.

第二课　在小吃部

甲：同志[1]，有[2]甜面包吗？

乙：有啊。你要营养面包还是奶油面包？

甲：一样一个[3]吧！

乙：还要什么[4]？

甲：再[5]来[6]碗[7]豆浆。

乙：还要别的吗？

甲：不[8]要了，一共多少[9]钱？

乙：两毛[10]。

甲：（拿出钱来[11]）

乙：你这是一块钱[12]，找给[13]你八毛。

LESSON 2: VOCABULARY

二	**èr**	two
在	**zài**	to be somewhere, locate in.
同志	**tóngzhì**	polite term of address, comrade, person
甜	**tián**	sweet
面包（麵～）	**miànbāo**	bread
营养（營養）	**yíngyǎng**	nutritious, nutrition
还是（還～）	**háishi**	or, alternative question
奶油	**nǎiyóu＝huángyóu**	butter
个（個）	**ge**	a measure word, a general classifier
一样一个 （～樣～個）	**yíyàng yíge**	one of each＜one kind, one piece
再	**zài**	again
来（來）	**lái**	come, here used as a proverb
碗	**wǎn**	bowl, here used as a measure
别的	**biéde**	other (things)
一共	**yígòng**	altogether
多少	**duōshǎo**	how much, how many
钱（錢）	**qián**	money
块钱（塊錢）	**kuài qián**	unit of money, yuan, dollar
两（兩）	**liǎng**	two
毛	**máo**	unit of money, 10 cents or 10 fen
拿	**ná**	to take
出…来(～…來)	**chū … lai**	come out, directional complement
这（這）	**zhè** or **zhèi**	this

是	shì	to be, copula verb
找，找钱（～錢）	zhǎo, zhǎoqián	to change, to change money
给（給）	geǐ	to give
八	bā	eight
豆浆（～漿）	dòujiāng	soybean milk

DÌ SĀN KÈ

ZÀI SHÍTÁNG (yī)

Jiǎ: Aiya! Zěnme zěnme jǐ? Hái děi páiduì.

Yǐ: Dōu shí-èr diǎn le, zhèngshi chīwǔfàn de shíhou.

Jiǎ: Jīntian yǒu shénme cài?

Yǐ: (kànkan càipái) O, yǒu hóngshāo yú, liū ròupiàr, làzi ròudīng, jīdàn bōcài fěnsī, xiāmi báicài.

Jiǎ: Wǒ tǐng xǐhuan chī báicài de.

Yǐ: Nà wǒ jiù yào ge hóngshāo yú, zánmen kěyǐ huǒzhe chī.

Jiǎ: Hǎo, xiān ná wǎn ba.

Yǐ: Zánmen dào dì èr chuāngkǒu páiduì, nàr rén shǎo.

LESSON 3

IN THE DINING HALL (One)

A: Oh, how come it's so crowded? We even have to wait in line.

B: It's already twelve o'clock, just lunch time.

A: What dishes are there today?

B: (*look at the menu board*) Oh, there's red-cooked fish, fried pork slices, diced chilli pork, egg, spinach with vermicelli, and shredded dried shrimp with cabbage.

A: I like cabbage a lot.

B: Then I'll have the red-cooked fish. We can share our dishes.

A: Okay, let's get some bowls first.

B: Let's line up at the second window. There're fewer people there.

第三课　在食堂（一）

甲：哎呀[1]，怎么[2]这么挤，还得[3]排队。

乙：都十二点[4]了，正是吃午饭的时候。

甲：今天有什么菜？

乙：（看看[5]菜牌）哦，有红烧[6]鱼，溜肉片，辣子肉丁，鸡蛋菠菜粉丝，虾米白菜……。

甲：我挺喜欢吃白菜的。

乙：那我就要个红烧鱼，咱们可以伙着吃。

甲：好，先拿碗吧。

乙：咱们到第二窗口排队，那儿人少。

LESSON 3: VOCABULARY

三	sān	three
食堂	shítáng	dining hall
这么（這麼）	zhènme or zènme	so, such manner
哎呀	aiya	gosh, oh!
挤（擠）	jǐ	crowded, to crowd
得	děi	must, to have to
排队（～隊）	páiduì	to form a line, to queue up
十二点钟（～～ 點鐘）	shí èr diǎn (zhōng)	twelve o'clock (shí-èr = ten plus two)
正是	zhèng shi	just, precisely
午饭（～飯）	wǔfàn	lunch, noon meal
时候（時～）	shíhour	time
菜	cài	side dishes, vegetables
菜牌	càipái	menu board (often posted or hung on the wall)
红烧（紅燒）	hóngshāo	red-cooked
鱼（魚）	yú	fish
溜	liū	fry, things coated with corn-starch
肉片儿（～兒）	ròupiàr < ròu + piàn	pork slices
辣子肉丁	làzi ròudīng	diced pork with chilli
鸡蛋（雞～）	jīdàn	egg
菠菜	bōcài	spinach
粉丝（～絲）	fěnsī	bean-flour noodle
虾米（蝦～）	xiāmǐ	dried shrimp
白菜	báicài	cabbage
挺	tǐng	very, very much, topmost
喜欢（～歡）	xǐhuan	to like

咱们（～們）	zánmen	we, us, inclusive: you and I or we
可以	kěyǐ	can, may
伙着	huǒzhe	to share, in company with
先	xiān	first
窗口	chuāngkǒu	window, kǒu is an opening
那，那儿（～兒）	nà, nàr	there
人	rén	person
少	shǎo	few, little

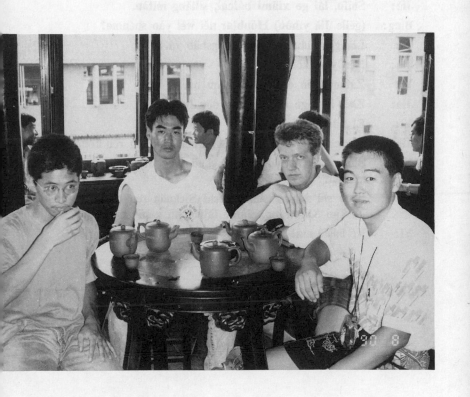

DÌ SÌ KÈ

ZÀI SHÍTÁNG (èr)

Jiǎ: Shīfu, lái ge xiāmi báicài, sìliǎng mǐfàn.

Bǐng: (gěile Jiǎ yǐhòu) Hòubiar nèi wèi yào shénme?

Yǐ: Liǎngge mántou, yíge hóngshāo yú.

Jiǎ: Nèr yǒu kōngwèi.

Yǐ: Zánmen jiù dào nèibiar qù ba.

Jiǎ: Zhèi liǎngge cài wèidao dōu búcuò.

Yǐ: Ê! búcuò shi búcuò, yú xiánle diǎr.

Jiǎ: Wǒ chīzhe zhèng héshī.   Nǐmen nánfāng rén kǒuqīng.

Yǐ: Shì a! Guài bude rénjia shuō "nán tián běi xián, dōng là xī suān" ne!

Jiǎ: Shuō shi zènme shuō, kěshi Sìchuān rén chīde cái là ne. Nǐ kàn Xiǎowáng, jiànle làjiāo jiù xiàng méi mìng shi de.

Yǐ: Kě búshì ma!

LESSON 4

IN THE DINING HALL (Two)

A: Chef, I'll have cabbage with dried shrimp and two bowls of rice.

C: (*after serving A*) And you behind there, what do you want?

B: Two steamed buns and a red-cooked fish.

A: There's an empty table over there.

B: Let's go over there.

A: Hey, these two dishes taste quite good.

B: Hm, they're okay, but the fish is a bit salty.

A: It tastes just right for me, you southerners like food to be bland, don't you?

B: That's right. No wonder people say "southern (food is) sweet, northern (food is) salty, eastern (food is) spicy and western (food is) sour."

A: That's what people say alright, but Sichuan people eat really spicy food. You should see Xiaowang, whenever he sees chilli peppers he goes crazy.

B: Isn't that so?

第四课 在食堂（二）

甲：师傅，来¹个²虾米白菜，四两米饭。

丙：（给了甲以后）后边儿那位要什么？

乙：两个馒头，一个红烧鱼。

甲：那儿³有空位。

乙：咱们就到那边儿去⁴吧。

甲：这两个菜味道都⁵不错。

乙：嗯，不错是不错⁶，鱼咸了点儿。

甲：我吃着⁷正合适，你们南方人口轻⁸。

乙：是啊！怪不得⁹人家说，南甜北咸，东辣西酸¹⁰呐。

甲：说是这么说，可是四川人吃的才辣呐¹¹。你看小王，见了辣椒就¹²象没命似的¹³。

乙：可不是吗！

四	sì	four
师傅（師～）	shīfu	chef, master
两（兩）	liǎng	1/10 of a jin, about 50 grams.
米饭（～飯）	mǐfan	rice
以后（～後）	yǐhòu	after, afterwards
后边儿（後邊儿）	hòubiar = hòu + biān	behind, at the back < back + side
位	wèi	polite classifier for persons
两个（兩個）	liǎng ge	two (pieces)
馒头（饅頭）	mántou	steamed bun (buns)
空位，空位子	kōngwèi, = kōngwèizi	free place, empty seats
那边儿（～邊儿）	nèibiar = nà + biān	over there = that side
味道	wèidao	taste, flavour, smell
不错（～錯）	búcuò	not bad, quite good
嗯	êg	Hm - expression of attention
咸（鹹）	xián	salty
一点儿（～點儿）	yì diǎr = yī + diǎn	a little
合适（～適）	héshì	suitable
你们（～們）	nǐmen	you (plural)
南方	nánfāng	the south, the southern part
南方人	nánfāngren	southerners
口轻（～輕）	kǒuqīng	bland (taste, palate)
= 口味轻	= kǒuwèi + qīng	
啊	a	particle of confirmation seeking agreement, suggestion, explanation

怪不得	guàibùde	no wonder (lit. can't blame)
人家	rénjia	people, others
说（說）	shuō	to say, to speak
南甜北咸 （～～～鹹）	nán tián běi xián	South is sweet, north salty
东辣西酸 （東～～～）	dōng là xī suān	east spicy, west sour. A set phrase of parallel construction meaning: Southerners like sweet food, Northerners like salty food, Easterners spicy and Westerners sour.
呐	ne	particle of confirmation, continuation, calling attention to variation of facts; rhetoric or emphatic interrogative.
可是	kěshi	but
四川	Sìchuān	Szechuan Province, in southwest China.
才	cái	really (is), emphatic adverb for "then and only then."
见	jiàn	to see
象（像）	xiàng	to be like
象…似的 （像～～）	xiàng … shide	as if it were …
没命	méimìng < méiyou mìng	to risk one's life
可不是吗 （～～～嗎）	kěbushì ma?	isn't that so?

ZAÌ SHÍTÁNG (sān)

Jiǎ: Zāole, tāng hēde tài duō chī búxiàle.

Yǐ: Jīntiān shīfu gěide tǐng duō de.

Jiǎ: Bǎ shèngxiàde dài huíqu, miǎnde làngfèi.

Yǐ: Zhèi bǐjiào hé nǐde kǒuwèi, liúzhe wǎnshang chī ba.

Jiǎ: Yě hǎo, hái shǎo xǐ ge wǎn ne!

Yǐ: Nà wǒ jiù bǎ zhèi sānge wǎn náqu xǐ, xǐwánle gē zài yíkuàr ma?

Jiǎ: Bǎ wǒ nèige gē zài zuì kào biār de wǎnjiàshang.

Yǐ: Xíng.

LESSON 5

IN THE DINING HALL (Three)

A: Oh no, I've had too much soup, I can't eat any more.

B: Today the chef gave us quite a lot.

A: Take the leftovers home so they won't be wasted.

B: This suits your palate better; save it for tonight.

A: Okay, I even have one bowl less to wash.

B: I'll just take these three bowls to wash; afterwards shall I put them away together?

A: Place mine on the end shelf.

B: All right.

第五课　在食堂（三）

甲：糟了，汤喝得太多[1]吃不下[2]了。

乙：今天师傅给得挺多的。

甲：把[3]剩下的带回去[4]，免得[5]浪费。

乙：这比较[6]合你的口味，留着[7]晚上吃吧。

甲：也好，还少[8]洗个碗呐！

乙：那我就把[9]这三个碗拿去洗，洗完了[10]搁在一块儿吗？

甲：把我那个搁在[11]最[12]靠[13]边儿的碗架上。

乙：行。

LESSON 5: VOCABULARY

糟了	zāole	golly! (exclamation) (lit. what a mess)
喝	hē	to drink
太	tài	too
多	duō	much, many
下	xià	down, get down, here used as result of the preceding verb **chī**, hence can't eat any more
把	bǎ	pre-transitive showing how an act is (to be) performed on the patient (object)
剩下的	shèngxià de	the leftovers, the remainder
带（帶）	dài	to take along, to bring, to carry
回去	huí (qù)	to return, to go back
免得	miǎnde	to avoid
浪费（～費）	làngfèi	to waste, extravagance
比较（～較）	bǐjiào	to compare, comparatively
合,适合(適～)	hé, shèhé	to suit, to satisfy
口味	kǒuwèi	taste, palate
留（留）	liú	to keep, to remain
也	yě	also
洗	xǐ	to wash
拿去	ná qu	to take (away)
完	wán	to finish
搁（擱）	gē	to put, to lay
一块儿（～塊 兒）	yíkuar = yī + kuài	together
那个（～個）	nèige = nà + yí + ge	that one

	= 那一个	
最	**zuì**	the most
靠	**kào**	leaning against, right next to
边的（邊～）	**biānde = biārde**	to the side
= 边儿的(邊兒～)		
架，架子	**jià, jiàzi**	shelf
行	**xíng**	all right

DÌ LIÙ KÈ

ZÀI PÉNGYOU JIĀ (yī)

Zhǔ Jiǎ: O, Dà Wáng láile.

Zhǔ Yǐ: Lái, lái, lái lǐbiar zuò.

Dà Wáng: Ng? Háizi ne?

Zhǔ Yǐ: Gēn xiǎo péngyou chūqu wár le; háizi ma, zài wūzili zǒng dāibuzhù.

Zhǔ Jiǎ: Dà Wáng, zěnme jīntian yǒu kòng chūlai zhuànzhuan?

Dà Wáng: Wǒ gāng xiěwán yì piān bàogào, chūlai huànhuan nǎojīn.

Zhǔ Yǐ: Dà Wáng, hē bēi chá ba; zhèi chá shì gāng qǐde, shāowéi děngyiděng.

Zhǔ Jiǎ: Xiān chōu zhī yān ba.

Dà Wáng: Nǐ wàngle ma, wǒ shi bù chōuyān de.

Zhǔ Jiǎ: Nà jiù chī kuài qiǎokèlì ba.

Dà Wáng: Zhèi chá hē qǐlai yǒu gǔ qīngxiāng wèr. Shì huāchá ma?

Zhǔ Yǐ: Shì Lìxíng chūchāi de shíhou cóng Hángzhōu dài huílái de Xīhú Lóngjǐng.

LESSON 6

AT A FRIEND'S HOME (One)

Host A: Oh, Dawang is here.

Host B: Come in, come in. Have a seat.

Dawang: Eh? Where is the little one?

Host B: She's gone out to play with her friends; you know kids, they can never stay inside for long.

Host A: Dawang, how is it that you have the time to come out?

Dawang: I just finished writing a report and came out to have a rest.

Host B: Dawang, have a cup of tea. It's just been made, you have to wait a while.

Host A: Have a cigarette first.

Dawang: Have you forgotten? I don't smoke.

Host A: Then have a piece of chocolate.

Dawang: This tea has a delicate fragrance. Is it jasmine tea?

Host B: It's the Longjing tea Lixing brought back from Hangzhou while on a business trip.

第六课　在朋友家（一）

主甲：哦，大王来了。

主乙：来，来，来里边儿坐[1]。

大王：嗯，孩子呢？

主乙：跟[2]小朋友出去玩儿了。孩子嘛，在屋子里总呆不住。

主甲：大王，怎么今天有空[3]出来转转？

大王：我刚写完一篇报告，出来换[4]换脑筋。

主乙：大王，喝杯[5]茶吧。这茶是刚泡的[6]，得稍微等一等。

主甲：先抽支烟吧。

大王：你忘了吗，我是不抽烟的。

主甲：那吃块巧克力吧。

大王：这茶喝起来[7]有股清香味儿，是花茶吗？

主乙：是力行出差的时候[8]从杭州带回来的[9]西湖龙井。

LESSON 6: VOCABULARY

六	**liù**	six
朋友	**péngyou**	friend
家	**jiā**	home, family
哦	**ò**	oh (exclamation)
大王	**Dàwáng** = Dà + Wáng	**Dà**, big **Wáng**, surname
里边儿（裏邊儿）	**lǐbiar** = lǐ + biān + r	inside
坐	**zuò**	sit down
孩子	**háizi**	child, children, term of endearment
小	**xiǎo**	little, small
玩儿（～儿）	**wár** = wán + r	to play, to have a good time
嘛	**me**	final particle expressing obviousness, 'as you know'
屋子	**wūzi**	room
总是（總～）	**zǒng shi**	always, constantly
呆不住	**dāi-buzhù**	cannot stay put
空	**kòng**	free time
转转（轉轉）	**zhuànzhuan**	to go out (lit. to turn around)
刚才（剛～）	**gāng cái**	just now
写（寫）	**xiě**	to write
（一）篇	**(yī) piān**	a measure word, classifier for compositions, poems, etc.
报告（報～）	**bàogào**	report
换换	**huànhuan**	to rest, to change, here used interchangeably with **xiēxie**
脑筋（腦～）	**nǎojīn**	brain
稍微	**shāowēi**	for a moment (dialect form)

杯，一杯	bēi, yībēi	cup, glass, also a classifier
茶	chá	tea
泡	pào	to steep
得	děi	should, must
等一等	děng yiděng	to wait a while
烟（煙）	yān	cigarette
抽烟（～煙）	chōu-yān	to smoke
支＝一支	zhī＝yīzhi	measure word for stick-like things, **zhī** is a classifier
忘	wàng	to forget
块（塊）	kuài	a measure word, piece, lump
巧克力	qiǎokèlì	chocolate
起来（～來）	qǐlai	an adverbial phrase used after a verb indicating action has taken place.
股	gǔ	classifier for fragrance, smell etc.
清香	qīngxiāng	light fragrance
味儿（～兒）	wèr＝wèi＋r	aroma, flavour
花茶	huāchá	jasmine tea, a kind of green tea
力行	Lìxíng	name
出差	chūchāi	to go on a business trip (for a subordinate who is on public service to say)
从（從）	cóng	from
杭州	Hángzhōu	Hangzhou (Hangchow)
西湖	Xīhú	West Lake
龙井（龍～）	Lóngjǐng	a famous brand of green tea (lit. Dragon Well)

DÌ QĪ KÈ

ZÀI PÉNGYOU JIĀ (èr)

Dà Wáng: Zěnme, zuìjìn máng bumáng?

Zhǔ Jiǎ: Zhèige yuè yǒu yìpī xuésheng lái chǎngli xuéxí, wǒmen děi duō chōu-chu shíjiān lai bāngzhù tāmen.

Dà Wáng: Zhèi yí jìdù de shēngchǎn gǎode zěnmeyàng?

Zhǔ Jiǎ: Bǐ shàng liǎng jìdù hǎoduōle.

Dà Wáng: Zhèipī xuésheng shì nǎr láide?

Zhǔ Jiǎ: Yǒude shi Wànfāng tāmen xuéxiàode, yǒude shi Gōngyè Dàxuéde.

Zhǔ Yǐ: Wǒmen nèi jǐge xuésheng zài xuéxiào zhuānyè dōu xuéde búcuò.

Zhǔ Jiǎ: Zài chǎngli biǎoxiàn de yě hěn hǎo.

Dà Wáng: Zènme shuōlai, xuéxiào gēn gōngchǎng guàgōu háishi yǒu tā hǎo de yímiàn. Tīngshuō guówài de lǐgōng xuéyuàn yě yǒu lèisì de bànfǎ.

Zhǔ Yǐ: Kě bushì ma?

LESSON 7

AT A FRIEND'S HOME (Two)

Dawang: How are things? Have you been busy recently?

Host A: This month a group of students came to the factory to do practical study, so we had to spend extra time to help them.

Dawang: How is this quarter's production going?

Host A: Much better than the previous two quarters.

Dawang: Where is this group of students from?

Host A: Some are from Wanfang's school and some are from the Industrial University.

Host B: Those students of ours did very well in their courses at school.

Host A: Their performance at the factory is also very good.

Dawang: So, co-operation between schools and factories does have its positive side. I have heard that Institutes of Technology overseas also have similar schemes.

Host B: There you are.

第七课　在朋友家（二）

大王：怎么，最近[1]忙不忙？

主甲：这个月有[2]一批学生来厂里学习，我们得多抽出时间来帮助他们。

大王：这一季度的生产搞[3]得怎么样？

主甲：比上两季度好多了。

大王：这批学生是哪儿来的？

主甲：有的是万芳她们学校的，有的是工业[4]大学的。

主乙：我们那几个学生在学校专业都学得不错。

主甲：在厂里表现得也很好。

大王：这么说来，学校跟工厂挂钩倒是[5]有它好的一面。听说国外[6]的理工学院[7]也有类似[8]的办法。

主乙：可不是吗。

LESSON 7: VOCABULARY

七	**qī**	seven
最近	**zuìjìn**	recently
忙	**máng**	busy
月	**yuè**	month, moon
一批	**yìpí**	a group
学生（學～）	**xuésheng**	student
厂，工厂（～廠）	**chǎng, gōngchǎng**	factory
学习（學習）	**xuéxí**	to study, to do practical training
抽出	**chōuchu**	to manage
时间（時間）	**shíjiān**	time, more formal than **shíhour** (Lesson 3)
抽出时间（～～時間）	**chōuchu shijian**	to manage to find time
教	**jiāo**	teach
季度	**jìdù**	a quarter (of a year)
生产（～產）	**shēngchǎn**	production, to produce
搞	**gǎo**	to do
怎么样（～麼樣）	**zěnmeyàng**	how (note: the **zěnme** in the first sentence of this lesson is a shortened form of **zěnme-yàng.**)
比	**bǐ**	compared with
上	**shàng**	last, previous
哪儿（～兒）	**nǎr**	where
学校（學～）	**xuéxiào**	school
工业（～業）	**gōngyè**	industrial, industry
大学（～學）	**dàxué**	university

专业（專業）	**zhuānyè**	speciality, course for professional training
表现（～現）	**biǎoxiàn**	performance
很	**hěn**	very
说来（說來） ＝说起来	**shuōlai＝shuōqilai**	following your talk, in that case
挂钩（掛鈎）	**guàgōu**	link up, hook up
倒是	**dàoshi**	actually, really
听说（聽說）	**tīngshuō**	hear (say)
国外（國～）	**guówài**	outside China
理工	**lǐgōng** ＝likē＋gōngkē	science and engineering
学院（學～）	**xuéyuàn**	institutes, colleges (university level)
类似（類～）	**lèisì**	similar
办法（辦～）	**bànfǎ**	method, way

DÌ BĀ KÈ

ZÀI PÉNGYOU JIĀ (sān)

Xiǎopíng:	Māma, māma!
Dà Wáng:	Xiǎopíng huílaile.
Zhǔ Yǐ:	Xiǎopíng, nǐ kàn shéi láile.
Xiǎopíng:	Wáng shūshu hǎo!
Dà Wáng:	Yì liǎngge yuè bújiàn jiù zhǎngde zènme gāole. Yòuéryuán āyí hǎo buhǎo?
Xiǎopíng:	Hǎo, āyí jiāo wǒmen chànggē tiàowǔ.
Zhǔ Yǐ:	Gěi Wáng shūshu chàng ge gēr.
Xiǎopíng:	Wǒ chàng ge "Yáng Liǔ Shù" hǎo ma?
Dà Wáng:	Hǎo.
Xiǎopíng:	(chàng)
Dà Wáng:	Hǎo jíle. O! shíhou bùzǎole, wǒ gāi zǒule. Xiàcì wǒ zǎodiǎr lái kàn nǐ tiàowǔ.
Zhǔ Yǐ:	Chīle fàn zài zǒu ma!
Dà Wáng:	Tài wǎn le, shāngdiàn yào guānmén le, wǒ hái děi qù mǎi xiē dōngxi. Xiàcì zài lái chīfàn.
Zhǔ Jiǎ:	Jìrán nǐ yǒushì. Nà wǒmen jiù bù qiáng liú le. Yǐhòu yǒu kòngr yídìng yào lái chī dùn biànfàn.
Zhǔ Yǐ:	Xiǎopíng, gēn Wáng shūshu shuō "zàijiàn".
Xiǎopíng:	Wáng shūshu zàijiàn.
Dà Wáng:	Zàijiàn, zàijiàn.
Zhǔ Jiǎ: Zhǔ Yǐ:	Mànzǒu, mànzǒu.

LESSON 8

AT A FRIEND'S HOME (Three)

Xiaoping: Mummy, mummy!

Dawang: Xiaoping is back.

Host B: Xiaoping, look who's here.

Xiaoping: Uncle Wang, how are you?

Dawang: I haven't seen you for a couple of months and you've grown so much. Do you like your teachers at the kindergarten?

Xiaoping: Yes, they've taught us to dance and sing.

Host B: Sing a song for Uncle Wang.

Xiaoping: How about "The Willow Tree"?

Dawang Good.

Xiaoping: (*sings*)

Dawang: Very good. Oh, it's getting late, I have to go now. Next time I'll come earlier so I can see you dance.

Host B: Have dinner with us before you go.

Dawang: It's getting late, the stores will be closed soon and I still have to buy a few things. I'll come for dinner next time.

Host A: Since you're busy we won't insist then. Next time you must come and have a meal with us when you are free.

Host B: Xiaoping, say goodbye to Uncle Wang.

Xiaoping: Goodbye Uncle Wang.

Dawang: Goodbye.

Host A:
Host B: So long.

第八课　在朋友家（三）

小平：妈妈[1]，妈妈！

大王：小平回来了[2]。

主乙：小平，你看谁来了？

小平：王叔叔好。

大王：一两个月[3]不见就[4]长得这么高了，幼儿园阿姨
　　　好不好？

小平：好。阿姨教我们唱歌跳舞。

主甲：给王叔叔唱个[5]歌儿。

小平：我唱个《杨柳树》好吗？

大王：好

小平：（唱）

大王：好极了！时候不早了，我该[6]走了。下次我早点儿[7]来看你跳舞。

主乙：吃了饭再[8]走嘛。

大王：太晚了，商店要关门了[9]，我还得[10]去买些东西。下次来再吃饭。

主甲：既然[11]你有事，那我们就不强留了，以后[12]有空儿一定要来吃顿便饭。

主乙：小平，跟王叔叔说"再见"。

小平：王叔叔再见。

大王：再见，再见。

主甲：
主乙：慢走，慢走。

LESSON 8: VOCABULARY

八	**bā**	eight
妈妈（媽媽）	**māma**	mummy
谁（誰）	**shúi** *or* **shéi**	who
叔叔	**shūshu**	uncle
长（長）	**zhǎng**	to grow
高	**gāo**	tall, high
幼儿园 （～兒園）	**yòuéryuán**	nursery school, kindergarten
阿姨	**āyí**	aunty
教	**jiāo**	to teach
唱，唱歌儿 （～～兒）	**chàng, chànggēr**	to sing, to a sing song
跳舞	**tiàowǔ**	to dance
杨柳（楊～）	**yángliǔ**	willow
树（樹）	**shù**	tree
好极了 （～極～）	**hǎo jíle**	very good, excellent (**ji**＝highest, extreme, cf. **tǐng** in Lesson 3)
走	**zǒu**	to walk, to leave
早＝早点儿 （～點兒）	**zǎo＝zǎodiěr**	early
下次，下一次	**xiàcì, xiàyīcì**	next time
该（該） 应该（應該）	**gāi, yīnggāi**	should, ought to, must
商店	**shāngdiàn**	shop, store
关门（關門）	**guān mén**	to close (lit. close door)
买（買）	**mǎi**	to buy
强留（～留）	**qiángliú**	insisting on, persuading somebody to stay

一定	**yídìng**	certainly, certain
便饭（～飯）	**biànfàn**	a meal (lit. convenient meal, i.e. simple meal)
再见（～見）	**zàijiàn**	goodbye
慢走	**mànzǒu**	goodbye, take care (lit. walk slowly)

DÌ JIǓ KÈ

ZÀI TÚSHŪGUǍN (yī)

Jiǎ: Nǐ shàng nǎr qu?

Yǐ: Wǒ shàng túshūguǎn qu jiè běn shū.

Jiǎ: Zhèr de túshūguǎn zài nǎr? Wǒ hái méi qùguo ne.

Yǐ: Nǐ hái méi qùguo a? Yào buyào wǒ gēn ni yíkuàr qù kànkan?

Jiǎ: Ò, nà tài hǎo le.

Yǐ: Zhèr lóuxià shi Zhōngwén shū, lóushàng shi wàiwén shū, shū dào tǐng quán de. Nǐ xiǎng kàn shénme shū dōu kěyǐ jiè.

Jiǎ: Yǒu shénme shǒuxù?

Yǐ: Gēn bié de dìfang chàbuduō. Xiān chá shūmù, shūmùguì jiù zài nèr.

Jiǎ: Zhèi shūmù shìbushi zuòzhě gēn shūmíng fēnkāi pái de?

Yǐ: Duìle, zuòzhě gēn shūmíng shi fēnkāi pái de.

Jiǎ: Shì zhào Pīnyīn pái de háishi zhào hànzì bǐhuà pái de?

Yǐ: Wǒmen zhèr zhǐ zhào Pīnyīn pái. Cháqǐlai gèng fāngbiàn xiē.

LESSON 9

AT THE LIBRARY (One)

A: Where are you going?

B: I'm going to the library to borrow a book.

A: Where's the library in this area? I still haven't been there yet.

B: Oh! You haven't been there? Would you like to come with me to have a look?

A: Sure, that would be great.

B: The Chinese books are downstairs and the foreign language books are upstairs. We have quite a good collection. You can borrow whatever book you like to read.

A: What do I have to do?

B: It's more or less the same as elsewhere. First check the catalogue; the catalogue cabinet is just over there.

A: Is this catalogue also arranged separately according to authors and titles?

B: Right, authors and titles are arranged separately.

A: Is it arranged according to Pinyin or according to character strokes in Chinese?

B: Here we only go by Pinyin. It's more convenient when looking up (a book).

第九课　在图书馆（一）

甲：你上[1]哪儿去？

乙：我上图书馆去借本书。

甲：这儿的图书馆在哪儿？我还没去过[2]呐。

乙：你还没去过啊！要不要我跟你一块儿去看看？

甲：哦，那太好了。

乙：这儿楼下[3]是中文书，楼上是外文书。书倒[4]挺全的。你想看什么书都[5]可以借。

甲：有什么手续[6]？

乙：跟别的地方差不多[7]，先查书目，书目柜就在那儿。

甲：这书目是不是作者跟书名分开[8]排的？

乙：对了，作者跟书名是分开排的。

甲：是照[9]拼音排的还是照汉字笔划排的？

乙：我们这儿只照拼音排，查起来[10]更方便些。

LESSON 9: VOCABULARY

九	jiǔ	nine
上	shàng	to go to, go up, a pro-verb
图书馆 （圖書館）	túshūguǎn	library
借	jiè	to borrow, to lend
书（書）	shū	book
本，一本	běn, yīběn	a measure word for books
楼下（樓～）	lóuxià	downstairs
中文	zhōngwén	Chinese language
楼上（樓～）	lóushàng	upstairs
外文	wàiwén	foreign language
全	quán	complete, whole
想	xiǎng	like to, want to, think of
手续（～續）	shǒuxù	procedure, regulations
地方	dìfang	place
差不多	chàbuduō	more or less the same
查	chá	check, look up
书目（書～）	shūmù	catalogue (of books)
柜，柜子 （櫃，櫃～）	guì guìzi	cabinet
照	zhào	according to
作者	zuòzhě	author
书名（書～）	shūmíng	book-title
分开（～開）	fēnkāi	separate, separately
排	pái	to arrange
对了（對～）	duìle	yes (agreement), correct
拼音	pīnyīn	pīnyīn, Chinese Romanization

汉字（漢～）	hànzì	Chinese characters
笔划（筆劃）	bǐhuà	strokes
只	zhǐ	only
更	gèng	more (for second degree of comparison)
方便	fāngbiàn	convenient
些，一些	xiē, yìxiē	a bit

DÌ SHÍ KÈ

ZÀI TÚSHŪGUǍN (èr)

Yǐ: Wǒmen dào shūkù qù kànkan qu.

Jiǎ: Zhèr shū hái zhēn bùshǎo ne!

Yǐ: Hái yǒu hǎo dà yí bùfen hái méi biānhào, dōu zài lóushàng yīcéng, nèixiē hái bùnéng jiè. Xiān kàn jiàzishang de ba.

Jiǎ: Ò, zhè shi fēnlèi bǎi de: zìrán kēxué, yīyào wèishēng, wénhuà jiàoyù, wénxué yǔyán, zhéxué lìshǐ, Mǎ liè zhǔyì jīngdiǎn zhùzuò.

Yǐ: Wǒ zhǎozhao wǒ yào de nèiběn shū, kàn yǒu méiyou.

Jiǎ: Shénme shū a?

Yǐ: Lǐ Shízhēn de Běncǎo Gāngmù.

Jia: Ò, nèi shǔyú yīyào wèishēng. Zài dìwǔ pái jiàzishang.

Yǐ: Êi! Jiàzishang méiyǒu ne. Dàgài dōu gěi jiè chūqu le ba. Zánmen dào jièyuèchù qù wènwen qu.

LESSON 10

AT THE LIBRARY (Two)

B: Let's go to the stacks and have a look.

A: There're really so many books here.

B: The majority still haven't been catalogued, they're all on the next floor and can't be borrowed yet. Let's look at the ones on the shelves here first.

A: Oh, these are classified by subject: natural science, medicine and health, culture and education, literature and language, philosophy and history, the Marxist-Leninist classics.

B: Let me see if they have the book I want.

A: Which one?

B: Li Shizhen's "Outline of Medicinal Plants."

A: I see. That's under medicine and health. It's on the shelf of the fifth row.

B: Strange, it's not on the shelf. Probably all of the copies have been checked out. We can ask at the loan section.

第十课　在图书馆（二）

乙：我们到书库去¹看看去。

甲：这儿书还真不少呐！

乙：还有好大一部分还没编号，都在楼上一层²，那些还不能借。先看架子上的吧。

甲：哦，这是分类摆的：自然科学，医药卫生，文化教育，文学语言，哲学历史，马列主义经典著作。

乙：我找找我要的³那本书，看有没有。

甲：什么书啊？

乙：李时珍⁴的《本草纲目》。

甲：哦，那属于医药卫生。在第五排架子上。

乙：嗯，架子上没有啊，大概都给⁵借出去了吧。咱们到借阅处去问问去。

LESSON 10: VOCABULARY

十	**shí**	ten
书库（書庫）	**shūkù**	stacks (lit. storeroom for keeping books)
真	**zhēn**	really, real
部分	**bùfen**	part, section
编（編）	**biān**	to catalogue, to give a number to, to edit
号（號）	**hào**	number
层（層）	**céng**	measure for floor, storey (lit. layer)
分类（～類）	**fēnlèi**	to classify
摆（擺）	**bǎi**	to put
自然	**zìrán**	natural
科学（～學）	**kēxué**	science
医药（醫藥）	**yīyào**	medicine
卫生（衛～）	**wèishēng**	health
文化	**wénhuà**	culture
教育	**jiàoyù**	education
文学（～學）	**wénxué**	literature
语言（語～）	**yǔyán**	language
哲学（～學）	**zhéxué**	philosophy
历史（歷～）	**lìshǐ**	history
马（马克思）馬，馬～～）	**Mǎ (Mǎkèsī)**	Marx (Karl Marx)
列（列宁）（～，～寧）	**Liè (Lièníng)**	Lenin
主义（～義）	**zhǔyì**	doctrine, -ism
马列主义（馬～～義）＝马克	**Mǎlièzhǔyì ＝Mǎkèsī-Lièníng**	Marxism-Leninism

思列宁主义 （马～～～宁～ 义）	**zhǔyì**	
经典（經～）	**jīngdiǎn**	classics
著作	**zhùzuò**	works
找	**zhǎo**	to look for, to find
本草纲目 （～～～綱～）	**Běncǎo Gāngmù**	Outline of Medicinal Plants (The Compendium of Materia Medica)
属于（屬～）	**shǔyú**	belonging to, of the same class
大概	**dàgài**	probably, generally
借阅处 （～閱處）	**jièyuèchù**	checkout counter (lit. borrow- to-read-place)
问（問）	**wèn**	ask

DÌ SHÍYĪ KÈ

ZÀI TÚSHŪGUǍN (sān)

Yǐ: (bǎ jièshūtiáo dì gěi guǎnlǐyuán)
Tóngzhì, yǒu zhèibǎn shū ma?

Guǎnlǐyuán: Wǒ chácha kan. Dōu gěi jièchūqu le, xiàxīngqī jiù
yǒu daoqīde.

Jiǎ: Wǒ yě xiǎng jiè zhèibǎn shū.

Guǎnlǐyuán: Jièshūzhèng ne?

Jiǎ: Hái méi bàn.

Guǎnlǐyuán: Nà qǐng nín xiān tián ge biǎo, dēngjì yíxià.

Jiǎ: (tián le biǎo dìgěi guǎnlǐyuán)

Guǎnlǐyuán: Zhōngwén xì, Chén Yīpíng. (xiě zài kǎpiànshang,
gàile zhāng). Zhè shi nínde jièshùzhèng, xiànzài jiù kěyǐ jiè
le.

Jiǎ: Máfan nín le.

Guǎnlǐyuán: Bú kèqi.

LESSON 11

AT THE LIBRARY (Three)

B: (*hands his call slip to the clerk*)
Say, do you have this book?

Keeper: I'll check. They've all been checked out, but some are due back next week.

A: I'd also like to borrow this book.

Keeper: Where's your library card?

A: I haven't got one yet.

Keeper: Then please fill out a registration form first.

A: (*fills out the form and hands it to the clerk*)

Keeper: Chinese Department, Chen Yiping. (*writes on the card and stamps it*) Here's your library card, you can use it now.

A: Thanks a lot for your trouble.

Keeper: Don't mention it.

第十一课　在图书馆（三）

乙：　　　（把借书条递[1]给管理员）同志，有这本书吗？

管理员：我查查看。都给借出去[2]了，下星期就有到期的[3]。

甲：　　我也想借这本书。

管理员：借书证呢？

甲：　　还没办。

管理员：那请您先填[4]个表，登记一下[5]。

甲：　　（填了表递给管理员）

管理员：中文系，陈一平（写在卡片上[6]，盖了章）。这是您的借书证，现在就可以用了。

甲：　　麻烦您了。

管理员：不客气。

借书条 （～書條）	jièshūtiáo	call slip
递给（遞給）	dì gěi	to hand to, to pass something to someone
管理员（～～員）	guǎnlǐyuán	keeper, caretaker, clerk
星期	xīngqī	week
到期	dàoqī	become due < reach date
借书证 （～書證）	jièshūzhèng	borrow-book-certificate, library card
办（辦）	bàn	to arrange for, to do
请（請）	qǐng	please, (I) invite (you) to
您	nín	polite form of nǐ
表	biǎo	form, list
登记（～記）	dēngjì	to register, to enrol
一下	yíxià	once, a while, tentatively
系	xì	department (lit. a system).
卡片	kǎpiàn	a card
盖章（蓋～）	gài zhāng	to stamp a document (zhāng is a stamp or a seal)
用	yòng	to use
麻烦（～煩）	máfan	bother, trouble
不客气 （～～氣）	búkèqi	don't mention it (lit. don't have the air of a guest)

DÌ SHÍER KÈ

DǍ DIÀNBÀO

Jiǎ : Qiánmian bú jiùshi yōudiànjú le ma?
Wǒ xiān jìnqu bǎ diànbào dǎle zài shuō.

Yǐ : Ng! shìbushì hái děi yìchéng diànmǎr zài dǎ?

Jiǎ : Búyòng.
(zǒu jìn yōudiànjú)

Jiǎ : Fā zhèi diànbào dào Xīní děi duōshao qián?

Bǐng : Wǒ kànkan duōshao zì, lián dìzhǐ yígòng shíwǔ ge zì, yígòng
shi sān kuài sì máo.

Jiǎ : Jīntian jiù néng dào ma?

Bǐng : Pǔtōng diànbào dōu néng dào, gèng búyòng shuō jiājí diànbào le.

Jiǎ : Nà tài hǎo le.

LESSON 12

SENDING A CABLE

A: Isn't that the Telegraph Office just ahead?
I'll go and send a telegram first.

B: Oh! Say, doesn't it have to be translated into telegraphic code before it's sent?

A: It's not necessary.
(*enters the Telegraph Office*)

A: How much will it cost to send this telegram to Sydney?

C: Let me see how many words there are.
Including the address there are fifteen words altogether, that's three dollars forty cents.

A: Will it get there today?

B: Even an ordinary telegram would make it, not to mention an urgent one.

A: That's great.

第十二课　打电报

甲：前面不就是邮电局了吗[1]？我先进去把电报打了再说[2]。

乙：嗯，是不是还得[3]译成电码再打？

甲：不用。

（走进邮电局）

甲：发这电报到悉尼得多少钱[4]？

丙：我看看多少字，连[5]地址十五个字，一共是三块四毛[6]。

甲：今天就能到吗？

丙：普通电报都[7]能到，更不用说加急电报了。

甲：那太好了。

LESSON 12: VOCABULARY

打	**dǎ**	to send (a telegram/cable)
电报（電報）	**diànbào**	telegram
前面	**qiánmian**	in front, ahead
邮电局(郵電～)	**yóudiànjú**	telegraph office
进去（進～）	**jìnqu**	to enter
嗯	**ng**	particle (exclamation)
译成（譯～）	**yìchéng**	translate into
电码（電碼）	**diànmǎ**	telegraphic code
发（發）	**fā**	to send out
字	**zì**	word, character
连（連）	**lián**	including
地址	**dìzhǐ**	address
普通	**pǔtōng**	ordinary, common
都	**dōu=(lián) . . . dōu**	even
能	**néng**	can, to be able to
加急	**jiājí**	urgent, express

DÌ SHÍSĀN KÈ

ZÀI YÓUJÚ

Jiǎ: Tóngzhì, zhèi fēng xìn wǒ xiǎng jì guàhào.

Yǐ: Shì shuāngguà háishi dānguà?

Jiǎ: Shénme jiào "shuāngguà" a?

Yǐ Shuāngguà jiùshi shōuxìn rén zài shōujù shang qiān le míng yǐ-hòu zài gěi jì huílai.

Jiǎ: Yào shuāngguà ba, děi duōcháng shíjiān cái dào?

Yǐ: Kōngyóu háishi píngyóu?

Jiǎ: Jì hángkōng.

Yǐ: Wǒ kàn, Kūnmíng—liǎngtiān jiù dào.

Jiǎ: Ò, yǒu jìniàn yóupiào ma?

Yǐ: Yǒu a, nǐ yào jǐ fēn de?

Jiǎ: Lái yì zhāng bāfēnde.

Yǐ: Bāfēn de yǒu nóngjù huà hé tǐyù de, nǐ yào shénme yàngr de?

Jiǎ: Liǎngyàng dōu tǐng hǎo de, yàobu yíyàngr lái yì zhāng ba.

LESSON 13

AT THE POST OFFICE

A: Excuse me, I want to send this letter by registered mail.

B: Double-registered or single-registered?

A: What is double-registered?

B: Double-registered means after the receipt is signed by the recipient it is sent back to you.

A: I'll have the double-registered then. How long will it take to arrive?

B: Airmail or surface mail?

A: Send it by airmail.

B: Let's see, to Kunming—it'll arrive in two days.

A: Say, are there any commemorative stamps?

B: Sure, what denomination would you like?

A: One eight-cent stamp.

B: For the eight-cent ones, we have pictures of agricultural tools and of athletics, which kind do you want?

A: They're both very nice, I'll take one of each.

第十三课　在邮局

甲：同志，这封信我想寄[1]挂号。

乙：是双挂还是单挂？

甲：什么叫双挂啊？

乙：双挂就是收信的人在收据上签了名，以后再给[2]寄回来。

甲：要双挂吧，得多长时间才到？

乙：空邮还是平邮？

甲：寄航空。

乙：我看，昆明——两天就到。

甲：哦，有纪念邮票吗？

乙：有啊，你要几分的？

甲：来一张八分的。

乙：八分的有农具画和体育的，你要什么样儿的？

甲：两样都挺好的，要不一样儿来一张吧。

LESSON 13: VOCABULARY

邮局（郵～）	**yóujú**	post office
封	**fēng**	classifier for letters, telegrams
信（信）	**xìn**	letter
寄	**jì**	send
挂号（掛號）	**guàhào**	register (mail parcels or letters)
双挂（雙掛）	**shuāngguà** = shuāng + guàhào	return registered < double registration
单挂（單掛）	**dānguà** = dān + guàhào	ordinary registered < single registration
叫	**jiào**	to be called, to be named
收	**shōu**	to receive, to keep
收据（～據）	**shōujù**	receipt
签（簽）	**qiān**	to sign
名，名字	**míng, míngzi**	name
多长时间（～長時間）	**duōcháng shíjiān**	how long, how much (time)
空邮（～郵）	**kōngyóu**	airmail
平邮（～郵）	**píngyóu**	ordinary mail, surface mail
航空	**hángkōng**	aviation
纪念（紀～）	**jìniàn**	commemorative, to commemorate
邮票（郵～）	**yóupiào**	stamps
分	**fēn**	unit of money, a cent
张（張）	**zhāng**	measured word for paper or other flat surface objects
昆明	**Kūnmíng**	Kunming, capital of Yunnan Province
农具（農～）	**nóngjù**	farm tools, agricultural instruments

画（畫）	huà	picture, painting
体育（體～）	tǐyù	athletics < physical training
样，样儿，样子 （樣，樣兒， 樣～）	yàng, yàngr, yangzi	form, shape, appearance

SHÀNG DIÀNYĬNG YUÀN

Jiǎ: Zhè shi Běijīng zhǎnlǎnguǎn, lǐbiar hái yǒu jùchǎng, diànyǐngyuàn ne. Nǐ xiǎng buxiǎng kàn diànyǐng?

Yǐ: Kànkan yǎn shénme piānzi.

Jiǎ: Jīntian gāng kāishǐ yǎn Àodàlìyà piān "Xīnwén Zhànxiàn".

Yǐ: Ò, nà hǎo, wǒ cónglái hái méi kànguo Àodàlìyà piānzi ne.

Jiǎ: Wǎnchǎng yǐjīng mǎnle, jiù zhǐ yǒu liǎng diǎnzhōng de le.

Yǐ: Zánmen jiù xiān bié qù dòngwùyuán kàn xióngmāo le, gǎi tiān
zài qù.

Jiǎ: (duì shòupiàoyuán) Yào liǎngzhāng piào.

Shòupiàoyuán: Yǒu yìmáo de yě yǒu liǎngmáo de.

Jiǎ: Yào liǎngmáo de hǎo le.

Jiǎ: Piào mǎihǎole.

Yǐ: Jǐpáide?

Jiǎ: Wǒ kànyikàn. Shísānpái shíbāhào, èrshíhào.

Yǐ: Hái yǒu shíjǐ fēnzhōng, xiànzài kěyǐ jìnqu le.

LESSON 14: VOCABULARY

GOING TO THE MOVIES

A: This is the Beijing Exhibition Hall, and inside there's a theatre and a cinema. Would you like to see a movie?

B: Let's see what movie is on.

A: The Australian film "Newsfront" just started today.

B: Oh good, I've never seen an Australian film before.

A: The evening show is already sold out, and there're only seats for the two o'clock show left.

B: Then let's not go to the zoo to see the pandas. We'll go there some other time.

A: (*to the ticket seller*) I want two tickets.

Ticket seller: There are 10-cent and 20-cent tickets.

A: I'll just take the 20-cent ones.

A: We've got the tickets.

B: Which row?

A: Let me see, thirteenth row, number 18 and number 20.

B: There's still a few minutes, we can go in now.

第十四课　上电影院

甲：　　这是北京展览馆[1]，里边儿还有[2]剧场、电影院呢，你想不想看电影？

乙：　　看看演[3]什么片子。

甲：　　今天刚开始演澳大利亚片《新闻战线》。

乙：　　哦，那好，我从来还没[4]看过澳大利亚片呐。

甲：　　晚场已经满了，就只有两点钟的啦。

乙：　　那咱们就先别[5]去动物园看熊猫了，改天再去。

甲：　　（对售票员）要两张票。

售票员：有一毛的，也有两毛的。

甲：　　要两毛的好了。

甲：　　票买好了。

乙：　　几排的？

甲：　　我看一看。十三排十八号、二十号。

乙：　　还有十几分钟，现在可以进去了。

电影（電～）	**diànyǐng**	movie, movie-film = electric shadows
电影院（電～～）	**diànyǐngyuàn**	cinema, movie theatre
展览（～覽）	**zhǎnlǎn**	exhibition
馆（館）	**guǎn**	hall
剧场（劇場）	**jùchǎng**	theatre
演	**yǎn**	to perform, to act
片，片子	**piān, piānzi**	film, movie
刚（剛）	**gāng**	just now
开始（開～）	**kāishǐ**	to begin
澳大利亚（～～～亞）	**Aòdàlìyà** *or* **Aòdàliyǎ**	Australia, Australian
新闻（～聞）	**xīnwén**	news < newly heard
战线（戰綫）	**zhànxiàn**	battle line, front
从来···没（從來···～）	**cónglái méi** *or* **cónglái bù**	never (always followed by negatives)
场（場）	**chǎng**	measure word for session, **wǎnchǎng** = evening show; a location, a place, theatre
满	**mǎn**	full
别	**bié**	don't (cf. **bíede** in Lesson 2)
动物园（動～園）	**dòngwùyuán**	zoo (lit. animal's garden)
熊猫（～貓）	**xióngmāo**	panda
改天	**gǎitiān**	to change a day, another day
售票员（～～員）	**shòupiàoyuán**	ticket seller
排	**pái**	row
开演（開～）	**kāiyǎn**	to start performing, showing
进去（進～）	**jìnqu**	go in
号（號）	**hào**	number

DÌ SHÍWǓ KÈ

ZÀI DIÀNYǏNGYUÀN

Shòupiàoyuán: Piào ne?

Jiǎ: Liǎng ge rén.

Jiǎ: Wǒmen de shì shuānghào, cóng yòubiar jìn.

Yǐ: Shì lóushàng háishi lóuxià?

Jiǎ: Lóuxià.

Yǐ: Zhè wèizi bù qián bú hòu, hái bú cuò.

Jiā: Jiùshi piānle diǎr.

Yǐ: Zhèi diànyǐngyuàn néng zuò duōshao rén?

Jiǎ: Dàgài yìqiān shàngxià ba, wǒ yě búdà qīngchu.

Jiǎ: Ò, dēng hēile, yào kāiyǎnle.

Yǐ: Yǒu méiyou jiāpiār?

Jiǎ: Yǒu xīnwén jiǎnbào.

LESSON 15

AT THE MOVIES

Ticket collector: Tickets?

A: Two people.

A: Ours are even numbers. We enter from the right.

B: Upstairs or downstairs?

A: We're downstairs.

B: These seats are neither too far forward nor too far backward. They're just right.

A: Only a bit to the side.

B: What's the seating capacity of this theatre?

A: Probably about a thousand, I'm not too sure.

A: See, the lights are dimming, it's about to start.

B: Are there any shorts?

A: There's a short news-reel.

第十五课　在电影院

收票员：　票呢？

甲：　　　两个人。

甲：　　　我们的是双¹号，从右边儿进。

乙：　　　是楼上还是楼下？

甲：　　　楼下。

乙：　　　这位子不前不后²，还不错。

甲：　　　就是偏了点儿。

乙：　　　这电影院能坐多少人？

甲：　　　大概一千上下³吧，我也不大清楚。

甲：　　　哦，灯黑了⁴，要开演了。

乙：　　　有没有加片儿⁵？

甲：　　　有新闻简报。

收票员 （～～員）	**shōupiàoyuán**	ticket collector
双号（雙號）	**shuāng (hào)**	even (number), pair
从（從）	**cóng**	from
右边儿（～邊兒）	**yòubiar =** **yòu + biān**	right (side)
位子	**wèizi**	seat, position
偏	**piān**	to the side
坐	**zuò**	to seat, to sit
大概	**dàgài**	about, approximately
千	**qiān**	thousand
上下	**shàngxià**	approximately, about
清楚	**qīngchu**	clear, clearly
灯（燈）	**dēng**	lights, lamps
黑	**hēi**	dark, black, darken
加片儿（～～兒）	**jiāpiàr (piān)**	extra films < shorts
简报（簡報）	**jiǎnbào**	short report, bulletin

KÀNWÁNLE DÌANYǏNG

Jiǎ: Zhèi piānzi de qíngjié bìng búxiàng yìbān de gùshìpiān.

Yǐ: Jiùshi, kànle bàntiān wǒ háishi mò míng qí miào, dàole yíbàr wǒ cái zhīdao shi zěnme huí shì.

Jiǎ: Búguò, zhōngwén zìmù dào hěn kǒuyǔhuà.

Yǐ: Qìxiān wǒ bìng bùdǒng "Newsfront" shi shénme yìshi. Hòulai cái zhīdao shi xīnwén gōngzuò rényuán zài cǎifǎng xīnwén shí suǒ jīngguò de dòuzhēng.

Jiǎ: Duìle. Jiù xiàng zài zhànchǎngshang shìde.

Yǐ: Zhèi dǎoyǎn kě zhēn bǎ ta xíngxiànghuà le.

Jiǎ: Zánmen zhēn yīnggāi duō kànkan lèisì de piānzi.

Yǐ: Shì a, zhǐ kěxī shàngyǎn de wàiguó piān tài shǎo le.

LESSON 16

AFTER THE MOVIE

A: The plot in this movie isn't like that of other feature films at all.

B: That's right.   After watching it I was still in the dark for quite awhile!   It was not until we were halfway through that I realized what it really was about.

A: Yet the subtitles were actually quite colloquial.

B: At first I didn't know what the meaning of "Newsfront" was. Later on I realized that it was about the struggles the newsmen went through when they were gathering news.

A: That's right.   It's as if they were on the battlefront.

B: The director has portrayed it well.

A: We really ought to see more of this kind of film.

B: Yes.   The only pity is that there are so few foreign films being shown.

第十六课　看完了电影

甲：这片子的情节并不象[1]一般的故事片。

乙：就是，看了半天[2]我还是莫名其妙[3]，到了一半儿才知道是怎么回事儿。

甲：不过，中文字幕倒[4]很口语化。

乙：起先我并不懂 NEWSFRONT 是什么意思，后来[5]才知道是新闻工作人员在采访新闻时所[6]经过的斗争。

甲：对了，就象在战场上似的[7]。

乙：这导演可真把它形象化[8]了。

甲：咱们真应该多[9]看看类似的片子。

乙：是啊，只可惜[10]上演的外国片太少了。

LESSON 16: VOCABULARY

情节（～節）	qíngjié	plot
一般	yìbān	ordinary, general, common
故事片	gùshìpiān	feature film
半天	bàntiān	a long time < half a day
莫名其妙	mò míng qí miào	unable to make head or tail of something
一半儿（～～兒）	yíbàr = yī + bàn	one half, middle
知道	zhīdao	know, realize
回事，一回事儿（～～～兒）	huíshì, yìhuíshìr	one thing (affair)
不过（～過）	búguò	but
字幕	zìmù	subtitles (lit. word screen)
倒	dào	actually, really, contrary
口语化（～語～）	kǒuyǔhuà	colloquialized
起先	qǐxiān	in the beginning, at first
并	bìng	emphatic adverb before negative
懂	dǒng	understand, comprehend
意思	yìsì	meaning, idea
后来（後來）	hòulái	later, afterwards
工作	gōngzuò	work
人员（～員）	rényuán	members, personnel
采访（採訪）	cǎifǎng	gather (news), collect data
所	suǒ	that (which)
经过（經過）	jīngguò	pass by, experience
斗争（鬥爭）	dòuzhēng	struggle
战场（戰場）	zhànchǎng	battlefield
导演（導～）	dǎoyǎn	(film or drama) director

形象化	**xíngxiànghuà**	depicting with images, portray
可惜	**kěxī**	regrettable, regrettably
外国（～國）	**wàiguó**	foreign countries, outside countries

DÌ SHÍQĪ KÈ

DǍ DIÀNHUÀ (yī)

Jiǎ: Tóngzhì, nǎr yǒu diànhuà?

Yǐ: Lóuxià yǒu.

Jiǎ: Zhèr de diànhuà shi zěnme dǎ de?

Yǐ: Dǎ nèixiàn háishi dǎ wàixiàn?

Jiǎ: Wàixiàn.

Yǐ: Dǎ wàixiàn děi xiān bō líng zài bō hàomǎr. Yàoshi dǎ nèixiàn zhíjiē bō jiù xíngle.

Jiǎ: Xièxie.

Jiǎ: Wèi, wèi, shi Běijīng Dàxué ma?
    Wǒ yào Zhōngwén-xì.

Jiǎ: Zhōngwén-xì ma? Qǐng ni zhǎo yíxià Lín Zhōng.

Bàngōngshì rényuán: Qǐng děng yíxià, wǒ qù kànkan.

Lí Zhòng: Wèi, shéi a?

Jiǎ: Lín Zhōng ma? Shì wǒ a! Míngtian wǎnshang yǒu diànyǐng "Xiǎo Huā" nǐ qù kàn ma?

Lín Zhōng: Shì gùshipiār ma?

Jiǎ: Shìde, tīngshuō hěn búcuò.

Lín Zhōng: Néng-bunéng duō gǎo yìliǎng zhāng piào? Wǒ kàn Qián Xiǎoróng tāmen yě xiáng qù, tāmen tǐng xǐhuan kàn diànyǐng.

Jiǎ: Zhè...wǒ xiǎng wèntí búdà.

Lín Zhōng: Nà wǒ jiù qu tongzhī tāmen.

Jiǎ: Míngtian wǎnshang qīdiǎn zài Rénmín Yǐngyuàn ménkǒur jiànmiàn.

Lín Zhōng: Jiù zhèyàng ba.

LESSON 17

MAKING A TELEPHONE CALL (One)

A: Excuse me, is there a telephone around here?

B: Downstairs.

A: How does one make a call?

B: Do you want an inside or outside line?

A: Outside.

B: For external calls first dial 'O' then the number. For internal calls just dial directly.

A: Thank you.

A: Hello, hello, is this Beijing University?
May I have the Chinese Department?

A: Is this the Chinese Department? May I speak to Mr Lin Zhong please?

Office personnel: Please wait a minute. I'll go and look.

Lin Zhong: Hello, who is it?

A: Is it Ling Zhong? It's me! Tomorrow evening there is a movie "Little Flower." Would you like to go?

Lin Zhong: Is it a feature film?

A: Yes, people say it's quite good.

Lin Zhong: Can you get a couple more tickets? I think Qian Xiaorong and his friend would like to go. They really like watching movies.

A: I think that will be all right.

Lin Zhong: Then I'll go and tell them.

A: I'll meet you at the entrance of the People's Cinema tomorrow evening at 7 o'clock.

Lin Zhong: That will do.

第十七课　打电话（一）

甲：　同志，哪儿有[1]电话？

乙：　楼下有。

甲：　这儿的电话是怎么打的[2]？

乙：　打内线还是打外线？

甲：　外线。

乙：　打外线得[3]先拨零，再拨[4]号码儿。要是打内线直接拨就行了。

甲：　谢谢。

甲：　喂喂，是北京大学吗？我要中文系。

甲：　中文系吗？请你找一下[5]林中。

办公室人员：请等一下，我去看看。

林中：喂，谁啊？

甲：　啊，林中吗？是我呀！明天晚上有电影《小花》，你去看吗？

林：　是故事片吗？

甲：　是的，听说很不错。

林： 能不能多搞两张票？ 我看钱小荣他们也想

去，他们挺喜欢看电影。

甲： 这……我想问题不大。

林： 那我就去通知他们。

甲： 明天晚上七点在人民影院门口儿见面。

林： 就这样吧。

电话（電話）	**diànhuà**	telephone
内线（～綫）	**nèixiàn**	internal line
外线（～綫）	**wàixiàn**	external line
拨（撥）	**bō**	to dial, to move
零	**líng**	zero
号码儿 （號碼兒）	**hàomǎr**	number (cf. **bian hào** in Lesson 10)
直接	**zhíjiē**	direct(ly)
谢谢（謝謝）	**xièxie**	thank you
喂喂	**wèi, wèi**	hello
等	**děng**	wait
办公室 （辦～～）	**bàngōngshì**	office
人员（～員）	**rényuán**	personnel
明天	**míngtian**	tomorrow
林中	**Lín Zhōng**	a personal name
小花	**Xiǎo Huā**	Little Flower, a personal name
问题（問題）	**wèntí**	problem, question
通知	**tōngzhī**	notify, inform
人民	**rénmín**	people, the masses
门口儿 （門～兒）	**ménkǒur**	entrance
见面（見～）	**jiànmiàn**	to meet < to see (each other's) face

DÌ SHÍBA KÈ

DǍ DIÀNHUÀ (èr)

Lín Zhōng: Shì Yīnyuè Xuéyuàn ma?

Diànhuàyuán: Shì de, nǐ zhǎo shéi?

Lín Zhōng: Qián Xiǎoróng zài buzài?

Diànhuàyuán: Hǎo, wǒ gěi nǐ zhǎo yíxia.

Diànhuàyuán: Tā yǒushì chūqule, xiàwǔ jiù huílai.   Nǐ yǒu shénme shì ma?

Lín Zhōng: Qǐng gàosu tā xiàwǔ gěi Běidà Zhōngwén-xì xìng Lín de dǎge diànhuà.

Diànhuàyuán: Xíng, xíng.

LESSON 18

MAKING A TELEPHONE CALL (Two)

Lin Zhong: Is it the Music Conservatory?

Receptionist: Yes. Who would you like to speak to?

Lin Zhong: Is Qian Xiaorong there?

Receptionist: I'll see if he's in.

Receptionist: He's out on business.   He'll be back in the afternoon.
               What can I do for you?

Lin Zhong: Please tell him to call Lin at the Chinese Depart-
               ment of Beijing University this afternoon

Receptionist: Okay.

第十八课 打电话（二）

林中： 是音乐学院吗？

电话员：是的，你找谁？

林： 钱小荣在不在？

电话员：我给[1]你找一下。

电话员：他有事[2]出去了，下午就回来。你有什么事吗？

林： 请告诉他下午给北大中文系姓林的[3]打个电话。

电话员：行，行。

LESSON 18: VOCABULARY

音乐（～樂）	yīnyuè	music
学院（學～）	xuéyuàn	institute
下午	xiàwǔ	afternoon
事，事情	shì, shìqing	thing, business
告诉（～訴）	gàosu	to tell
北大＝北京大學（～～學）	Běidà＝Běijīng Dàxué	Peking University
姓	xìng	surname
姓林的	xìng Lín de	a person named Lin

DÌ SHÍJIŬ KÈ

DǍ DIÀNHUÀ (sān)

Qián: Shì Lín Zhōng ma? Wǒ kàndao nǐde tiáor le, yǒu shénme shèr ma?

Lín: Zhào Fēng gǎodào le jǐzhāng "Xiǎo Huā" de piào, nǐ hé Sūn Xiǎotíng yào qù ma?

Qián: Něi tiān de?

Lín: Míngtian wǎnshang qīdiǎn bàn.

Qián: Míngtian shi xīngqīliù, wǎnshang dào méishìr.

Lín: Nà nǐ gàosu Sūn Xiǎotíng, wǒmen qīdiǎn zài Rénmín Yǐngyuàn ménkǒur pèngtóu.

Qián: Jiù zhèiyàng ba, xièxie nǐ le.

Lín: Zhè háiyòng xiè? Míngtian jiàn.

LESSON 19

MAKING A TELEPHONE CALL (Three)

Qian: Is that **Lin** Zhong? I saw your message.
      What's happening?

Lin: Zhao Feng managed to get a few tickets for "Little Flower,"
     do you and Sun Xiaoting want to go?

Qian: Which day is it for?

Lin: Tomorrow night at seven thirty.

Qian: Tomorrow is Saturday, I've nothing to do in the evening.

Lin: Then you tell Sun Xiaoting to meet us at seven o'clock **at**
     the entrance of the People's Cinema.

Qian: All right, we'll see you then. I ought to thank you.

Lin: What's there to be thanked for?
     See you tomorrow.

第十九课　打电话（三）

钱：是林中吗？我看到[1]你的条儿了，有什么事儿吗？

林：赵峰搞到了几张《小花》的票，你和孙小庭要去吗？

钱：哪天的？

林：明天晚上七点半[2]。

钱：明天是星期六，晚上倒没事儿。

林：那你告诉孙小庭，我们明天晚上七点在人民影院门口碰头。

钱：就这样吧，谢谢你了。

林：这还用谢[3]？明天见。

LESSON 19: VOCABULARY

条儿（條兒）	tiáor	a message, a note
赵峰（趙～）	Zhào Fēng	a personal name
孙小庭（孫～～）	Sūn Xiǎotíng	a personal name
哪天的	něitiānde＝nǎyì- tiānde	which day
半	bàn	half
星期六	xīngqīliù	Saturday (lit. the sixth day of the week)
碰头（～頭）	pèngtóu	to meet
用	yòng	need
明天见 （～～見）	míngtianjiàn	see you tomorrow

DÌ ÈRSHÍ KÈ

SHÀNG NĂR QU?

Lǐ: Xiǎo Chén, nǐ zènme cōngcōngmángmáng de shàng nǎr qù a?

Chén: Shàng huǒchēzhàn jiē rén.

Lǐ: Qù jiē shéi a?

Chén: Wǒ shànghuí gēn nǐ tíguo de nèige lǎo tóngxué, tā dào Guǎng-zhōu chūchāi, cóng zhèr lùguò.

Lǐ: Jǐdiǎn de chē?

Chén: Wǔshíèr-cì lièchē, bādiǎn yíkè dào.

Lǐ: Xiànzài zhǐ yǒu èrshíjǐ fēn zhōng le, zuò chē hái děi huàn yícì, kǒngpà láibují le, yàobu nǐ jiù qí wǒde chē qù ba.

Chén: Bùle, wǒ hài děi hé ta yìqǐ zuòchē huílai, wǒ xiǎng háishi jiào liàng chūzū qìchē qu hǎo yìdiǎr.

Lǐ: Nà jiù kuài zǒu ba.

LESSON 20

WHERE ARE YOU GOING?

Li: Xiaochen, where are you going in such a hurry?

Chen: To meet someone at the train station.

Li: Who are you meeting?

Chen: The old classmate whom I mentioned to you last time.   He is passing through here on a business trip to Canton.

Li: Which train is he on?

Chen: Number 52, It arrives at eight-fifteen.

Li: Now you have only about 20 minutes.   If you go by bus you will have to change buses once, I'm afraid you won't make it.   Why don't you take my bike?

Chen: No, thanks.   I have to come back with my friend by car. I think it would be better if I hired a taxi.

Li: In that case you had better hurry.

第二十课　上哪儿去？

李：小陈，你这么匆匆忙忙地[1]上哪儿去呀？

陈：上火车站接人！

李：去接谁呀？

陈：我上回跟你提[2]过的那个老同学，他到广州出差[3]，从这儿路过[4]。

李：几点的车？

陈：52次（列车），八点一刻到。

李：现在只有二十几分钟了，坐车还得换[5]一次，恐怕来不及了，要不[6]你就骑[7]我的车去吧。

陈：不了，我还得和他一起[8]坐车回来，我想还是叫[9]辆出租汽车去好一点儿。

李：那就快走吧。

LESSON 20: VOCABULARY

匆忙	**cōngmáng**	in a hurry
火车 (～車)	**huǒchē**	train
站	**zhàn**	station, a stop
接	**jiē**	to meet and welcome (somebody), to pick up someone, to receive
回	**huí**	measure word for happenings (cf. **húishì** in Lesson 16)
提过 (～過)	**tí-guo**	to mention, to raise, to bring up (a topic)
老	**lǎo**	old (time)
同学 (～學)	**tóngxué**	classmate, schoolmate
路过 (～過)	**lùguò**	en route, to pass through a place
列车 (～車)	**lièchē**	a train (several cars in a row)
一刻	**yíkè**	a quarter (of an hour)
坐车 (～車)	**zuò chē**	to go by cars or vehicles
换	**huàn**	to change, exchange
恐怕	**kǒngpà**	(I'm) afraid, probably
来得及(來～～) (不)	**lái (de) jí (bu)**	there (is) enough time to (isn't)
骑 (騎)	**qí**	to ride (bike, horse)
自行车(～～車)	**zìxíngchē**	bike
一起	**yìqǐ**	together (cf. **yíkuàir** in Lesson 1 and Lesson 9)
叫	**jiào**	to call
辆 (輛)	**liàng**	measure word for vehicles
出租汽车(～～車)	**chūzū qìchē**	taxi <car for hire
快	**kuài**	quick

DÌ ÈRSHÍYĪ KÈ

ZÀI HUǑCHĒZHÀN (yī)

Chén: Tóngzhì, cóng Shěnyáng lái de huǒochē tíng zài něige zhàntái?

Fúwùyuán: Shì wǔshíèr-cì ba? Yíhào zhàntái, zǎo jiù dàole.

Chén: Nà zěnme bàn ne? Zènme duō rén, sháng nǎr qù zhǎo a?

Fúwùyuán: Dào guǎngbōzhàn qù ràng guǎngbōyuán gěi jiào yíxià.

Chén: Tóngzhì, máfan nǐ gěi jiào yíxià cóng Shěnyáng láide Shěn Dàpéng zài hòuchēshì ménkǒur děng Chénwěi.

Guǎngbō: Lǚkèmen qǐng zhùyì. Cóng Shěnyáng láide Shěn Dàpéng qǐng dào hòuchēshì ménkǒur qù, yǒu rén zhǎo nǐ.

LESSON 21

AT THE TRAIN STATION (One)

Chen: Excuse me sir, which is the exit gate for the train from Shenyang?

Service assistant: Is that number 52? It's at gate number one. It arrived quite a while ago.

Chen: What can I do? Among all these people, where can I find him?

Service assistant: Go to the paging office and have them make an announcement.

Chen: Excuse me, can I trouble you to page Shen Dapeng from Shenyang to wait for Chen Wei at the entrance to the waiting room?

Announcer: Passengers, attention please. Would Shen Dapeng from Shenyang please go to the waiting room entrance. Someone is looking for you.

第二十一课　在火车站（一）

陈：　　　同志，从沈阳来的火车停[1]在哪个站台？

服务员[2]：是52次吧？一号站台，早就到了。

陈：　　　那怎么办呐？这么多人上哪儿去找啊！

服务员：到广播[3]站去让广播员给叫一下。

陈：　　　同志，麻烦你给叫一下从沈阳来的沈大朋在候车室门口等陈伟。

广播：　　旅客们请注意[4]！从沈阳来的沈大朋请到候车室门口儿去，有人找你。

LESSON 21: VOCABULARY

沈阳（瀋陽）	**Shěnyáng**	Shenyang, the capital of Liaoning Province
站台（～臺）	**zhàntái**	(station) platform
服务员（～服務員）	**fúwùyuán**	service assistant
怎么办（～麼辦）	**zěnme bàn**	what's to be done
广播（廣～）	**guǎngbō**	announce, broadcast
广播站（廣～～）	**guǎngbōzhàn**	announcement desk, paging office
广播员（廣～員）	**guǎngbōyuán**	announcer
让（讓）	**ràng**	to ask (somebody to do something), let
叫	**jiào**	to call (to page)
候车室（～車～）	**hòuchēshì**	waiting room (at a station)
旅客们（～～們）	**lǚkèmen**	passengers, travellers
注意	**zhùyì**	pay attention

Chén: Lǎo Shěn, wǒ láiwǎnle, ràng nǐ jiǔ děng le.

Shěn: Méishèr, wǒ yì chū zhàntái jiù tīngdao guǎngbō le.

Chén: Chē zuòle zènme jiǔ, lùshang xīnkǔ le ba?

Shěn: Hái hǎo, zài chēshang hái néng shuì yìhuèr.

Chén: Zǒu ba, chē zài nèibiar ne, wǒ lái gěi nǐ tí zhèige xiāngzi.

Shěn: Bù, bù, wǒ zìjǐ lái.
(Shàng le chē).

Shěn: Zhè shi Dōngběi de dàdòu, gěi nǐmen chángchang.

Chén: Aiya, nǐ dài zhème duō lai, guài máfan de.

Shen: Méi shénme. Yìsi yìsi.

— 130 —

LESSON 22

AT THE TRAIN STATION (Two)

Chen: Laoshen, sorry I'm late. I've made you wait so long.

Shen: Not at all. As soon as I came out of the gate, I heard the announcement.

Chen: You must be very tired after such a long trip.

Shen: It's alright, I was able to sleep on the train.

Chen: Let's go, the car is over there. Let me take the suitcase for you.

Shen: No, no, I'll carry it myself.
    (*they get into the car*)

Shen: Here're some soybeans from the Northeast.

Chen: Oh, you brought so much. Thank you.

Shen: Not at all. It's my pleasure.

第二十二课　在火车站（二）

陈：老沈，我来晚了，让¹你久等了。

沈：没事儿，我一出站台就²听到广播了。

陈：车坐了这么久，路上辛苦了吧？

沈：还好，在车上还能睡一会儿。

陈：走吧，车在那边儿呐，我来给你提这个箱子。

沈：不，不，我自己³来。

　　（上了车）

沈：这是东北的大豆，给你们尝尝⁴。

陈：哎呀，你带⁵这么多来怪⁶麻烦的。

沈：没什么，意思意思。

久	jiǔ	long (time)
一…就…	yì … jiù …	as soon as … then …
路上	lùshang	on the way, during the journey
辛苦	xīnkǔ	hard (ship), weary, tired
一会儿 （～會兒）	yìhuèr	a while (cf. yíxià in Lesson 11)
提	tí	to lift by hand (cf. Lesson 20)
箱子	xiāngzi	suitcase
自己	zìjǐ	self, oneself
东北（東～）	Dōngběi	the Northeast
大豆	dàdòu	soybeans
尝尝（嘗嘗）	chángchang	taste, try
带（帶）	dài	bring
怪	guài	extraordinary, extremely < strangely
意思意思	yìsi yìsi	a token

DÌ ÈRSHÍSĀN KÈ

ZÀI LÙSHANG

Chén: Xiān dào wǒ jiā qù háishi xiān dào lǚguǎn?

Shěn: Xiān dào lǚguǎn ānpái yíxià ba.

Chén: Sījī tóngzhì, qǐng kāi dào Hépíng Bīnguǎn.

Sījī: Bú jiùzài Wángfǔjǐng nàr ma? Hǎo.

Shěn: Jiāli zěnmeyàng?

Chén: Hái hǎo, háizi míngnián jiùyao shàng xiǎoxué le.

Shěn: Xiǎo Liú hái zài Běiyī Sānyuàn gōngzuò ba?

Chén: Duì, búguò tā shàngxīngqī gāng zǒu, gēn tāmen de yīliáoduì xiàxiāng qùle, yào sānge yuè hòu cái huílai.

Shěn: Nà, háizi ne?

Chén: Háizi lǎolao dài. Tā kě gāoxìng ne.

Shěn: Nǐ bǎ ta sòngdao Dàniáng nàr qu la?

Chén: Bù, bǎ lǎolao jiēlái le.

Shěn: Yǒu ge lǎorénjia zhàoliào shì hǎo.

Chén: O, dàole, xiàchē ba.

Chén: Shì yíkuài èr ba?

Sījī: Duìle. Gěi nín piào.

Shěn: Hǎo. Máfan nǐ.

Sījī: Méishénme, zǒu hǎo.

LESSON 23

ON THE ROAD

Chen: Should we go to my home or to the hotel first?

Shen: Let's go to the hotel and fix up things first.

Chen: Driver, please take us to the Peace Hotel.

Driver: It's right around Wangfujing, isn't it?
All right.

Shen: How is everybody at home?

Chen: Not bad, my child will be going to primary school next year.

Shen: Is Xiaoliu still working at Beiyi Sanyuan (the Peking Medical College Hospital No.3)?

Chen: Yes, but she just left last week to go to the countryside with her medical team, and won't be back for three months.

Shen: What about the child?

Chen: Grandma is looking after him. He's so excited.

Shen: You sent him to live with Grandma?

Chen: No, we have Grandma come and live with us.

Shen: It's good to have an older person around.

Chen: Oh, we are here. Let's get off.

Chen: A dollar twenty, isn't it?

Driver: Right. I'll give you a receipt.

Shen: Thank you.

Driver: Not at all. Goodbye.

第二十三课　在路上

陈：　　先到我家去还是先到旅馆？

沈：　　先到旅馆安排[1]一下吧。

陈：　　司机同志，请开到[2]和平宾馆。

司机：　不就在王府井那儿吗[3]？　好。

沈：　　家里怎么样？

陈：　　还好，孩子明年就要上小学了。

沈：　　小刘还在北医三院工作吧？

陈：　　对，不过她上星期刚走，跟她们的医疗队下
　　　　乡去了，要三个月后才回来。

沈：　　那，孩子呢？

陈：　　孩子姥姥[4]带，他可[5]高兴呢。

沈：　　你把他送到大娘[6]那儿去啦？

陈：　　不，把姥姥接来了。

沈：　　有个老人家[7]照料是好[8]。

陈：　　哦，到了，下车吧。

陈：　　是一块二吧？

司机：对了，给您票。

沈：　好。麻烦你。

司机：没什么。走好。

家	jiā	home (cf. **rénjiā** in Lesson 4)
旅馆（～館）	lǚguǎn	hotel
安排	ānpái	to arrange
司机（～機）	sījī	driver
开，开车（開，開車）	kāi, kāichē	to drive < to start a vehicle.
和平宾馆（～～賓館）	Hépíng Bīnguǎn	Peace Hotel (**bīnguǎn** = guest house)
王府井	**Wángfǔjǐng**	a place name
家里（～裏）	jiālǐ	home
那儿（～兒）	nàr	nearby, neighbouring area
明年	míngnián	next year
小学（～學）	xiǎoxué	primary school
北医三院＝北京医学院第三医院（～～醫學～～～醫～）	**Běiyī Sānyuàn** = **Běijīng Yīxuéyuàn Dìsān Yīyuàn**	Hospital No. 3. of the Beijing Medical College
医疗队（醫療隊）	yīliáoduì	medical team
下乡（～郷）	xiàxiāng	to go to the countryside
姥姥	lǎolao	(maternal) grandma
高兴（～興）	gāoxìng	happy
平时（～時）	píngshí	in normal times, on usual days
老人家	lǎorénjia	older person (respectful term)
照料	zhàoliào	to take care of, to look after
送到	sòngdao	send off, escort to
到了	dàole	arrived
走好	zǒu hǎo	goodbye (lit. walk carefully)

Shěn: Tóngzhì, you kōngfáng ma?

Fúwùyuán: Liǎngge rén?

Shěn: Bù, zhǐ wǒ yíge.

Fúwùyuán: Zhù jǐtiān?

Shěn: Sìwǔ tiān ba.

Fúwùyuán: Qǐng zài zhèr dēngjì yíxià.

Shěn: (tiánxiě) Fángfèi ne?

Fúwùyuán: Shàngmiàn yǒu shuōmíng.

Shěn: Huǒshìfèi ne?

Fúwùyuán: Lìngwài suàn.

Chén: Něige fángjiān?

Fúwùyuán: Sìlóu sì yāo èr.

Shěn: Zánmen zuò diàntī shàngqu bǎ dōngxi fàngxia, zài shàng
nǐ jiā, hǎo ma?

Chén: Zhèi fángjiān hái zhēn bù xiǎo ne!
Zǒu ba, shàng wǒ jiā qù chī wǔfàn.

Shěn: Zhè jiù zǒu.

LESSON 24

AT THE HOTEL

Shen: Hello, do you have any vacancies?

Clerk: Two people?

Shen: No, just myself.

Clerk: For how many days?

Shen: Four or five days.

Clerk: Please register here.

Shen: (*fills out the form*)
What is the rate?

Clerk: It's written on top.

Shen: Does it include meals?

Clerk: They're separate.

Chen: Which room?

Clerk: Fourth floor, room 412.

Shen: Let's take the elevator first and put away the things, and then go to your place. All right?

Chen: This room is really quite big! Come on, let's go home and have lunch.

Shen: I am coming.

第二十四课　在旅馆

沈：　　　同志，有空房吗？

服务员：　两个人？

沈：　　　不，只我一个。

服务员：　住几天？

沈：　　　四五[1]天吧！

服务员：　请在这儿登记[2]一下。

沈：　　　（填写）房费呐？

服务员：　上面有说明。

沈：　　　伙食费呢？

服务员：　另外[3]算。

陈：　　　哪个房间？

服务员：　四楼四一二。

沈：　　　咱们坐电梯上去把东西放下，再上你家，好吗？

陈：　　　这房间还真不小呐！走吧，上我家去吃午饭。

沈：　　　这就走[4]。

LESSON 24: VOCABULARY

空房	**kōngfáng**	vacancy (lit. vacant room)
住	**zhù**	stay, live
房费（～費）	**fángfèi**	room rates, tariff
说明（說～）	**shuōmíng**	to explain, explanation
伙食费 （～～費）	**huǒshífèi**	meals (lit. cost for the meals)
另外	**lìngwài**	separately, besides, extra
算	**suàn**	to calculate, to count
房间（～間）	**fángjiān**	room
一，幺（么）	**yāo**	one, an alternate pronunciation for yī.
放下	**fàngxia**	to put down, to lay down
上去	**shàngqu**	to go up
电梯（電～）	**diàntī**	lift, elevator
东西（東～）	**dōngxi**	things, objects

DÀOLE JIĀLI

Dàniáng: O, nǐmen huílai le!

Shěn: Dàniáng, ràng nín jiǔ děng le, wǒmen xiān dào lǚguǎn qùle yítàng.

Dàniáng: Dōu ānpái hǎole ma?

Shěn: Dōu hǎole.

Chén: Mā, nòng diǎr shénme chī ne?

Dàniáng: Bāo jiǎozi ba, děng huèr dào Lǐ jiā bǎ háizi jiē huílai.

Shěn: Suíbian chī diǎr shénme, búyào tài fèishì.

Dàniáng: Xiàr gēn miàn dōu huòhǎo le, dàhuǒr dòng shǒu bāo jiù chéng. Bú fèishì.

Shěn: Gǎn pír wǒ chéng, nǐmen bāo wǒ lái gǎn.

Dàniáng: Kàn nǐ gǎnde zènme kuàidang, zài jiā cháng bāo jiǎozi ba?

Shěn: Yě jiùshì féngnián guòjié, péngyou xiāngjù cái chī yí dùn.

Chén: Bāo de chàbuduō le, xiān zhǔzhe ba.

Dàniáng: Jiǎozi xià guō le, gāi qù jiē Xiǎoqīng le.

Chén: Duì, xǐ le shǒu jiù qù.

LESSON 25

ARRIVING HOME

Mother: Oh, you're back!

Shen: Ma'am, sorry we've kept you waiting.
We went to the hotel first.

Mother: Is everything arranged?

Shen: Everything's fine.

Chen: Mother, what shall we make?

Mother: Let's have dumplings. Later we're to go and pick up the child.

Shen: Anything will do. Don't go to a lot of trouble.

Mother: The filling and dough are ready. We'll do the wrapping together, there's nothing to it.

Shen: I'm quite good at rolling the dough. You wrap and I'll roll.

Mother: You're so quick at rolling, you must often have dumplings at home.

Shen: Only during the holidays or when we have gatherings with friends.

Chen: We've wrapped about enough. Let's boil these first.

Mother: The dumplings are being cooked now. You should go and bring Xiaoqing home.

Chen: I'll go as soon as I've finished washing my hands.

第二十五课 到了家里

大娘： 哦，你们回来了[1]。

沈： 大娘，让您久等了，我们先到旅馆去了一趟[2]。

大娘： 都安排好了吗？

沈： 都好了。

陈： 妈，弄点儿什么吃呐？

大娘： 包饺子吧。等会儿到李家把孩子接回来。

沈： 随便吃点什么，不要太费事。

大娘： 馅儿[3]跟面都和[4]好了，大伙儿动手包就成。不费[5]事。

沈： 擀皮儿我成，你们包我来擀。

大娘： 看你擀得这么快当，在家常包饺子吧？

沈： 也就是逢年过节[6]，朋友相聚才吃一顿。

陈： 包得差不多了，先煮着[7]吧。

大娘： 饺子下锅了，该去接小青了。

陈： 对，洗了手就去。

LESSON 25: VOCABULARY

大娘	**dàniáng**	polite term of address to an older lady
一趟	**yítàng**	measure for trips
弄	**nòng**	to do, to make
包	**bāo**	to wrap
饺子（餃～）	**jiǎozi**	dumplings
随便（隨～）	**suíbiàn**	as you wish, at your convenience, informally
费事（費～）	**fèishì**	take the trouble, to bother
馅儿（餡兒）	**xiàr**	filling
面	**miàn**	dough
和	**huò**	to mix together, to knead
大伙儿（～～兒）	**dàhuǒr**	in company, together
动手（動～）	**dòng shǒu**	to begin an action, to begin doing
成	**chéng**	it will be done; to be able
擀	**gǎn**	to roll out
快当（～當）	**kuàidang**	skilful and quick
逢年过节（～～過節）	**féngnián guòjié**	New Year and other festivals
朋友相聚	**péngyou xiāngjù**	gathering of friends
差不多	**chàbuduō**	almost, more or less
煮着	**zhǔzhe**	to be boiled
下锅（～鍋）	**xià guō**	put in the pot
手	**shǒu**	hands

PART TWO

GRAMMAR AND USAGE

Chinese utterances are usually spoken with a particle at the end to express the attitude of the speaker. These particles are called sentence final particles. The most common ones are: **a; ma; le; ne.** They are to be found in the notes.

The normal word order of a Chinese sentence is the same as that of English sentences *Subject Verb Object* except that Chinese makes use of the position of the noun in the sentence to distinguish definiteness from indefiniteness. So a noun in the subject position i.e. *at the front* of the sentence, is definite and a noun that is in the object position, i.e. *at the end* of the sentence, is indefinite. Thus, in order to focus on or make more "definite" nouns normally in the object position, one must use different devices to move them to the front of the sentence (i.e. to "prepose" it). One such device is the **bǎ** construction (see Note 3, Lesson 5); another is the *Topic and Com ment* construction (see Note 8, Lesson 4).

It is easier to ask a question in Chinese than in English. One can simply use a question word at the place in the sentence where the information is needed to make a declarative sentence. That is, Chinese questions take the same word order as do statements. In order to seek confirmation of, or answers to, yes or no types of question, one can either add the **ma** question particle to the statement or make the statement into a *positive + negative?* type of alternative question. Thus, the question form is Verb + **bù** + Verb? e.g. **nǐ lái bù lái?** (lit. You come not come?) "Are you coming?"

LESSON 1

1. **guò** 过: An aspect marker attached directly to verbs to indicate the completion of an action or past experience. This expression is often used as a form of greeting.

   As such, it is equivalent to:

   Chīle ma? 吃了吗? Have eaten?
   Chī fàn le ma? 吃饭了吗? Have eaten meal?
   Chī le fàn le ma? 吃了饭了吗? Have eaten meal?
   Chī guò fàn le ma? 吃过饭了吗? Have eaten meal?

   Notice that situational greetings such as this often lead naturally to discourse if the interlocator chooses to carry on with sentence as in the dialogue here. Otherwise, one can simply say,

   Chīle, nǐ ne?
   吃了，你呢? Yes, (I) have eaten. How about you?

2. **le** 了: There are two forms of **le**. This one is a sentence final modal particle indicating a changed or imminent change of situation.

   Shuìjiào le.
   睡觉了。
   Sleep + (modal particle)   It's time for bed.
   I'm going to sleep now.

   Guānmén le.
   关门了。
   Close door + (final particle)   (We're) closing now.

   Answers to "yes or no" questions use the same verb as indicated in the question whether in the positive or in the negative:

   Guānmén le ma? Guān le.
   关门了吗? 关了。 Is it closed? (Yes), it is closed.

   Guān le méi guān? Guān le.
   关了没关? 关了。 Is it closed? (Yes), it is closed.

3. **ma** 吗: Interrogative particle making a statement into a "yes or no" question.

   Nǐ chī fàn + ma?
   你吃饭+吗? Do you eat rice? or (a meal)?

Chī a.

吃啊。 Yes, I do.

Tā xìng Lǐ + ma?

他姓李+吗? Is his surname Li?

Shì de.

是的。 Yes, it is.

4. **dōu** 都: same as **yǐjīng** 已经 (already).

Tiān dōu hēi le, kuàidiǎnr huí jiā ba.

天都黑了，快点儿回家吧。

It's already dark; we'd better be getting home.

Dōu yì diǎn zhōng le, zěnme hái bù chī fàn?

都一点钟了，怎么还不吃饭?

It's already one o'clock; why aren't we eating?

Zhè xuéqī dōu kuài wán le; wǒ hái méi kāishǐ xiě bāogào ne!

这学期都快完了，我还没开始写报告呢！

This semester is almost over; (yet) I haven't even begun to write the report.

5. **méi** 没: A derivation from the negative aspect **bù** + **yǒu** 不 + 有 = **méiyǒu** 没有, where "**yǒu**" 有 is an aspect marker of verbs indicating the completion of an action, and functions just like the auxiliary verb "have" in English.

Tā chī fàn.

他吃饭。 He eats rice (or meal).

Tā méi (yǒu) chī fàn.

他没（有）吃饭。He hasn't eaten.

6. **a** 啊: sentence final particle. Its pronunciation is modified by the preceding syllable. If the preceding syllable ends in an open vowel such as **-a, -e, -i, -o, -u**, then it is **ia** 呀. If it ends in **-u** or in **-ao**, then it is **-ua** 哇. If it ends in **-n**, then it becomes **na** 哪（呐）, and all the others are pronounced **a** 啊.

As the most frequently used particle, its meanings are also wide ranging. The main use, however, is to tone down the voice of the utterance, making it sound less abrupt or brusque. Other uses are for greeting, commanding, warning, reminding, explaining, etc:

Kuài chī a, shítàng yào guān mēn le.

快吃啊，食堂要关门了。

Hurry up and eat, the dining room is closing.

Bù chī fàn qù shàngkè bù xíng a.

不吃饭去上课不行啊。

Going to class without eating just won't do.

Shéi a?

谁呀？

Who is it?

Xiǎo Qín a, lái a.

小勤呐，来呀。

Xiao Qin, come here.

7. de 得: Sentential complement marker indicating extent.
   Verb + de + complement:

   Chī de wǎn.

   吃得晚。

   Eat late.

   Chī de bù wǎn.

   吃得不晚。

   Didn't eat late.

   Shuìjiào shuì de zǎo.

   睡觉睡得早。

   Sleep early.

   Shuìjiào shuì de bù zǎo.

   睡觉睡得不早。

   Didn't sleep early.

   The complement is often expanded into a clause:

   Tā chī de bǎo de bù néng zǒu le.

   他吃得饱得不能走啦。

   He is so full that he can't walk.

   (He ate to the extent of being so full that he can't walk.)

8. Same construction as 7; here the complement marker **de** 得 is
   omitted as often happens in colloquial speech:

   Qǐlai wǎn le.

   起来晚了。 Got up late.

   Shuì zǎo le.

   睡早了。 Went to bed early. (Sleep early this time.)

9. **ng, en, e** 嗯: "Say" or "by the way", expressions calling for
   attention or showing attention.

10. Prepositional phrases, like other modifying phrases in Chinese, precede the head of their construction as in this sentence:

Dào shítáng qù.

到食堂去。　　Go to the dining hall.

When the phrase is followed by a clause as in this sentence, it has the same function as "to" when used in English for expressing purpose, as in the second "to" in ". . . going to the canteen to see if there is anything to eat . . .". Used in this way, **qù** 去 then becomes redundant and can be omitted without affecting the meaning of the sentence.

11. Verbs can be reduplicated to indicate tentativeness or momentariness, thus conveying suggestion rather than insistence. Many commands and requests are phrased in this manner.

Xǐxǐ shǒu zài chī fàn.

洗洗手再吃饭。

Wash your hands before you eat.　(See Note 5, Lesson 3)

12. a) **de** 的: Noun marker, making a verb into a noun.
    b) Question word + noun in object position indicates indefiniteness and arbitrariness in the noun.

Yǒu shénme chī de?

有什么吃的？

Is there anything to eat?

Yǒu shénme chī de méi you?

有什么吃的没有？

Is there anything to eat?

Answer: **Yǒu.** 有。　　Yes, there's.

　　　　Méiyǒu. 没有。　　No, there isn't.

13. **zhè** 这 = **zhèhuìr** 这会儿：This moment, right away.

14. **jiù** 就 + Verb indicates the action will take place momentarily.

Jiù qǐlai. 就起来。　　Will get up right away.

Jiù zǒu le. 就走了。　　Will be leaving soon.

15. **gēn** 跟: Conjunction "and," conjoining nouns but not verbs, except for certain foreignisms, thus the meaning "with," resulting in the same construction as in the prepositional phrases explained in Note 10 above.

Wǒ gēn tā yíkuàr chī fàn.

我跟他一块儿吃饭。

I eat with him (together).

16. **cái** 才: Then and only then, stressing certainty either positively or negatively.

17. **ne** 呐, 呢: Sentence final particle indicating obvious facts.

   Wǒ zuótiān wǎnshang shuì de cái hǎo ne.
   我昨天晚上睡得才好呢!
   I slept very well indeed last night (contrary to what you think).

   A marker of questions not of a yes-or-no type, to be added to interrogative sentences to seek particular information.

   Zhè shi shénme ne?
   这是什么呢?   What is this (anyway)?

   As a question marker, it can be added to nouns in a given context to mean "How about . . .?" "Where is . . .?"

   Tā qù, nǐ ne?
   他去, 你呢?   He is going, how about you?

   Wǒde shū ne?
   我的书呢?   Where is my book?

   Ne also indicates that an action is in the progressive state. In such sentences the verb often takes the **zhe** aspect marker.

   Tā shuìjiào ne.
   他睡觉呢。   He is sleeping.

18. **ba** 吧: Sentence final particle indicating request, command, suggestion, or tag question marker indicating assumption on the part of the speaker.

   Qù shuìjiào ba!
   去睡觉吧!   Go to sleep!

   Nǐ shuìjiào shuì de hǎo ba?
   你睡觉睡得好吧?   You slept well, didn't you?

19. **kě** 可: emphatic adverb.

   Tā kě méi qù.
   他可没去。
   He actually didn't go. (or) On the contrary, he didn't go.

20. **yào** 要: auxiliary verb, will, want to.

   Xiǎochībù yào guān mén le.
   小吃部要关门了。   The canteen will be closing soon.

   Wǒ yào xué zhōngwén.

我要学中文。　　I want to study Chinese.

21. The normal word order is **dùzi** è 肚子饿: Stomach is hungry or to be hungry. The reverse order here suggests the meaning of "to cause to be hungry."

22. Verb phrase + **ye** 也 + verb phrase 2: Whether or not the supposition contained in either verb phrase can be established, the consequence will be the same; hence the construction is sometimes preceded by **suíran** 虽然, (even) if.

LESSON 2

1. **Tóngzhì** 同志: Formal term of address for adults of either sex. The frequency of its use in urban society has extended the meaning to include the common noun "a person"; e.g.

   Tā shì ge nǚ tóngzhì.

   她是个女同志。　　She's a female (person).

   In rural or village society, however, kinship terms are more likely to be used as people know each other more intimately there, and strangers are rare enough to allow efforts to fit them into kinship patterns.

2. **Nouns** after yǒu 有 (have) are indefinite, thus this is a typical way to ask questions like:

   Nǐ yǒu . . . ma?

   你有…吗?　　Do you have any . . .? (Do you have some . . .?)

3. a) **ge** 个: Classifier for nouns. It is sometimes called measure words as they function like units when combined with a numeral or a demonstrative.

   Numeral (or Demonstrative) + classifier + noun

   zhè这, **nà** 那 + ge 个 + **wǎn** 碗

   yī 一, **èr** 二, **sān** 三, **sì** 四, **wǔ** 五
   liù 六, **qī** 七, **bā** 八, **jiǔ** 九, **shí** 十 + **wǎn**碗 + **dòujiāng**豆浆

   b) Distributive construction:

   Numeral + whole + numeral + classifier

   yì rén yí gè

   一人一个　one per person, or (one person one something)

   yì tiān sān cì

   一天三次　three times a day, or (one day, three times)

4. **Interrogative** sentences with question words: Unlike their counterparts in English, keep the same word order in Chinese in declarative and negative sentences.

   Zhè shì shénme? 这是什么?　　What is this?
   Tā shì shuí? 他是谁?　　Who is he?
   Zhèr shì nǎr? 这是哪儿?　　Where is this?
   Zhè zěnme zuò? 这怎么做?　　How to make this?

— 157 —

5. **zài** 再: This is an adverb for future action " . . . repeat doing something . . ." " . . . again" " . . . more . . ." used much like the French word *encore* adopted by English-speaking audiences for:

Qǐng nǐ zài shuō yí biàn.

请你再说一遍。

Please repeat once more. (Please say it one more time.)

Compare with another adverb **yòu** 又 which has a similar meaning except the action is already completed:

Tā yòu shuō le yí biàn.

他又说了一遍。 He said it once more.

6. **lái** 来: Pro-verb substituting verbs with concrete meaning.

Nǐ chī nèi ge, wǒ lái zhèi ge.

你吃那个，我来这个。 You have that one, I'll have this.

Xiāngzi tài zhòng le, wǒ lái.

箱子太重了，我来。 The suitcase is too heavy, let me take it.

Zài lái yí gè!

再来一个！ Encore!

7. **(yì) wǎn** （一）碗: Classifier or measure word which can mean "one" with the numeral "one" omitted.

8. **bù** 不: negative adverb; it is added immediately to the verb to negate it. When the verb is **you** 有 "have" or if the verb takes an aspect marker (**le** 了 "perfective" or **guo** 过 indefinite past") **bu** is changed to **méi (yǒu)** 没（有）"did not have."

Tā mǎi miànbāo.

他买面包。 He (wants to) buy bread.

Tā bù mǎi miànbāo.

他不买面包。 He doesn't (want to) buy bread.

Tā méiyǒu miànbāo.

他没有面包。 He doesn't have bread.

Tā mǎile miànbāo.

他买了面包。 He has bought (some) bread.

Tā méi (yǒu) mǎi miànbāo.

他没有买面包。 He didn't buy bread.

9. **duōshǎo** 多少: a compound made up of **duo** "many" + **shao** "few" and meaning "how much" when the compound is combined with stative verbs such as **gāo** 高, **cháng** 长, **zhòng** 重 etc.,

the second element **shǎo** is often dropped and the tone of the
first element **duō** is changed to the rising tone **duó**.

    Duō gāo   多高   how tall
    Duō cháng 多长   how long
    Duō zhòng 多重   how heavy

10. Chinese monetary units, like other units, are decimal:
    yī 1   **shí** 10 **bǎi** 100 **qiān** 1,000 **wàn** 10,000

èr 2		
sān 3	*units*	*Fractions*	*Objects*
sì 4	**fēn**	**bàn**	**qián**
wǔ 5	分 cents	半 half	钱 money
liù 6	**máo (jiǎo)**		
qī 7	毛(角) ten cents		
bā 8	**kuài**		
jiǔ 9	块 dollar		
shí 10			

    Note: In counting money, when fractions are included, omit
              the "**qián**."

11. Directional complements:
Motion verb + Direction (**lái** 来, **qù** 去) indicates the direction
of the motion.
lái 来: direction toward the speaker.
qù 去: direction away from the speaker.
Verbs which are directional in meaning may combine with **lai**
and **qu** to form compound directional complements.
Motion verb + compound directional complement

Ná	**chūlai**	**yíge miàobāo**
拿	出来	一个 面 包
Take	out	a roll (bread).

Mài	**chūqu**	**hěn duō (wǎn) dòujiāng**
卖	出去	很 多 （碗） 豆浆
(We)	sold (out)	a lot of soybean milk.

12. Substantive predicates are ordinarily used to clarify an identity:
Tā liùchǐ (gāo).
他六尺（高）。 He's six foot (tall).
Wǒ lǎo jiā Fújiàn
我老家福建。

I am from Fujian. (My ancestral home is Fujian.)

13. More examples of verb phrases with indirect objects: (See Note 1, Lesson 18)

A. Gěi tā dǎ diànhuà.
给他打电话。
Give him a phone call.

B. Dǎ diànhuà gěi tā.
打电话给他。
Make a phone call to him.

Zhǎo gěi tā wǔmáo qián.
找给他五毛钱
Give him 50 cents.

Zhǎo wǔmáo qián gěi tā.
找五毛钱给他
Give 50 cents to him.

Gěi tā xiě xìn.
给他写信
Write him a letter.

Xiě xìn gěi tā.
写信给他
Write a letter to him.

A & B are interchangeable, although A may also be benefative.

LESSON 4

1. Pro-verb **lái** 来: to have, to do, to get, to give, to take.
   Lái ge xiǎoyèqǔ. 来个小夜曲。 Let's have a serenade.

2. (**yī** +) classifier + noun: When **yī** is omitted it is an ellipsis form
   for one something.
   Yào wǎn niú ròu miàn.
   要碗牛肉面。 (I'll) have a bowl of beef noodles.
   Mǎi pánr hóng shāo ròu.
   买盘儿红烧肉。 (I'll) take a plate of "red-cooked" pork.
   Ná bēi pí jiǔ.
   拿杯啤酒。 (Get) a glass of beer.

3. Location markers are added to common and proper nouns to
   form place-nouns:

— 163 —

4. Preposition + place noun + direction verbs:

Dào fēijīchǎng qù. 到飞机场去.   To go to the airport.

Dào nèi biānr qù. 到那边去。   Go over there.

Dào zhèi biānr lái. 到这边来。   Come over here.

5. Marking plurality in the adverbial **dōu** 都:

Zhè liǎng běn shū dōu hěn yǒu yìsi.

这两本书都很有意思。   Both of these books are interesting.

Běifāngrén dōu ài chī jiǎozi.

北方人都爱吃饺子。   (All) Northerners love to eat jiǎozi.

Nánfāngrén dōu xǐhuān chī mǐfàn.

南方人都喜欢吃米饭。   (All) Southerners love to eat rice.

6. Concessive construction:

Hǎo shì hǎo, kěshì tài guì le.

好是好，可是太贵了。

It's alright but it's a bit expensive.

Other conjunctions which also mean *but*:

> **dànshì** 但是
>
> **búguò** 不过
>
> **jiùshì** 就是

Wǒ shì wánquán tóngyì nǐ, dànshì (búguò, jiùshì)...

我是完全同意你，但是（不过，就是）…

I agree with you all right, but...

7. zhe 着 is added to the verb to stress a particular point about the subject.

Chuānzhe zhèng héshì.

穿着正合适。   It's just right when you wear it.

8. Topic and comment or double subject constructions:

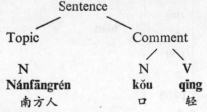

Nánfāngrén kǒu qīng.

南方人口轻。

As for Southerners, palate is bland.

(Southerners like bland food.)

Wǒ tóu téng.

我头痛。　　(As for me) my head aches.

Jīntian tiānr hǎo.

今天天儿好。　　It's a good day today.

Tā yǎn gāo shǒu dī.

他眼高手低。　　He has high aims but low abilities.

9. The conjunction **guài bù dé** 怪不得: no wonder

Tā nàme yònggōng, guài bù dé (tā) kǎo de nàme hǎo.

他那么用功，怪不得（他）考得那么好。

He's so diligent no wonder he got such a good grade.

Tā nàme hàochī, guài bù dé nàme pàng.

他那么好吃，怪不得那么胖。

He sure can eat, no wonder he's so fat.

Zhè tiānqì zhèmo hǎo, guài bù dé dàjiā dōu xǐhuān dào zhèr lái.

这天气这么好，怪不得大家都喜欢到这儿来。

It's such good weather here, no wonder everyone likes to come here.

10. Colloquial fixed expressions:

wǔ hú sì hǎi

五湖四海

five lakes, four seas (every corner of China)

dōng nán xī běi

东南西北

east, south, west, north (in all directions)

Zhāng Sān Lǐ Sì

张三李四

John Doe, Mary Brown (anybody)

gè fēn dōng xī

各分东西

each goes his own way

luàn qī bā zāo

乱七八槽

chaotic mess

zhāo Qín mù Chǔ

朝秦暮楚

Serving Qin in the morning and Chu in the evening

(quick to switch sides)

hú shuō bā dào

胡说八道

to talk nonsense

yì zhī bàn jiě

一知半解

half-baked knowledge

bànjìn bā liǎng

半斤八两

six of one and half a dozen of the other (the same thing)

mǎma hūhu

马马虎虎

Not precise

sān xīn èr yì

三心二意

indecisive; can not make up one's mind

yì xīn yí yì

一心一意

with great determination

quán xīn quán yì

全心全意

wholeheartedly

11. Conjunction **cái** 才 in Cai . . . Ne 才 … 呢: to indicate contrariness to what was said before.

Shuō de cái liúlì ne!

说得才流利呢! (He) actually speaks very fluently.

Xiǎng de cái duō ne.

想得才多呢。 (He) actually thinks a lot.

Huà de cái hǎo ne!

画得才好呢! (He) actually draws very well.

12. Conjunction **jiù** 就: Verb + **le** 了 . . . **jiù** 就 . . . to show cause and effect. Verb + ing . . . then . . . : le is the aspect marker indicating the completion of an action.

Jiànle tā jiù xiàng jiànle qīnrén sìde.

见了他就象见了亲人似的。

Seeing him is like seeing loved ones.

Jiàn xiàngpiān jiù xiǎng qǐ tā láile.

见了相片就想起他来了。

Looking at a picture, she thinks of him.

Jiànle táng jiù xiàng méi mìng sìde.

见了糖就象就没命似的。

Seeing candy, he cannot resist.

13. **Xiàng ... sìde** 象 ⋯ 似的 It's like ...

Tā shuō huà jiù xiàng chànggē sìde.

她说笑话就象唱歌似的。

The way she speaks is like singing. (Her voice is like music.)

Tā xiězì jiù xiàng huàhuàr sìde.

他写字就象画画似的。

His calligraphy is like painting.

Tā pǎo qǐlái jiù xiàng fēi sìde.

他跑起来就象飞似的。

He runs so fast that it's like flying.

Tā shuō xiàohua jiù xiàng zhēn de sìde.

他说笑话就象真的似的。

He tells jokes with a straight face.

LESSON 5

1. Sentential complement oɪ extent or manner. (See Note 7, Lesson 1)

Positive	Negative
Tā hējiǔ hēde tài duō.	**Hēde bú tài duō.**
他喝酒喝得太多。	喝得不太多
He drank too much.	Didn't drink much.
Tā xuéde hěn hǎo.	**Xuéde bù tài hǎo**
他学得很好。	学得不太好
He studied well.	Didn't study well.
Tīngde hěn qīngchù	**Tīngde bù qīngchù**
听得很清楚	听得不清楚
Heard it clearly	Didn't hear it clearly
Xiěde tài màn	**Xiěde bú tài màn**
写得太慢	写得不太慢
Wrote too slowly	Didn't write slowly
Zhǎngde tǐng hǎo kàn de	**Zhǎngde bù hǎo kàn**
长得挺好看的	长得不好看
He/she has grown to be quite goodlooking	Grown to be not so attractive

2. Verbs with potential complements — Verb + **de/bù** + complement — indicate result of the action. (See Note 5, Lesson 15)

chī de (bù) wán
吃得（不）完
can (can't) finish eating it

chī de (bù) xiāo
吃得（不）消
can (can't) take it

xiǎng de (bù) kāi
想得（不）开
can (can't) take things philosophically

3. Disposal construction introduced by subject, verb, object **bǎ** 把 +complement can be changed to the following form; S + **bǎ** 把 +O+V+complement/particle. It describes how an action

— 168 —

is carried out on the object and thus focuses on the latter.

Huàirén dǎ le tā.

坏人打了他。

The bad guy hit him.

Huàirén bǎ tā dǎ le.

坏人把他打了。

The bad guy beat him up.

Tā chīlè jiǎozi.

他吃了饺子。

He ate dumplings.

Tā bǎ jiǎozi chīle.

他把饺子吃了。

He ate the dumplings.

Bǎ zhè shìr miáoxiědé xiàng zhēndè.

把这事儿描写得象真的。

He described it to such an extent that it seemed real.

4. Directional complement: Verb + Direction. (See Note 4, Lesson 4)

Dài huìqu	带回去	take it back
fàng shànglai	放上来	put it up here
ná guòqu	拿过去	take it over there
ná jìnqu	拿进去	take it in
ná chūlai	拿出来	take it out
ná xiàlai	拿下来	bring it down
ná chūqu	拿出去	take it out (away from the speaker)

5. **miǎndé**, 免得: in order to avoid.

miǎndé bái pǎo yí tàng

免得白跑一趟　　so that I/he avoids going in vain

miǎndé tā bù gāoxìng

免得他不高兴　　so that he won't be unhappy

miǎndé chū shì

免得出事　　so that there won't be an accident

miǎndé fàn cuòwù

免得犯错误　　to avoid making mistakes

miǎndé dézuì rénjiā

免得得罪人家　　to avoid offending people

6. Comparisons:

Comparisons are best understood as having a qualifying phrase inserted in front of the unqualified stative verb (e.g. *to be + adjective* in English is a single stative verb in Chinese.) To state superior degrees, the qualifying phrase is **bǐ** 比 + obj. in comparison with the object.

Wǒ gāo 我高 "I am tall" is an unqualified statement. But **Wǒ bǐ tā gāo** 我比他高 "I am taller than he" is a qualified statement.

For additional emphasis, also insert an emphatic adverb **gèng** 更 (or **hái** 还): even... -er (or still... -er). e.g.

Wǒ bǐ tā gèng gāo. 我比他更高。 I am even taller than he.

Alternatively, additional emphasis can be expressed by the complement phrase... **de duō** ...得多 or ... **duō le** ... 多了 "much...-er" added after the stative verb, e.g.

Wǒ bǐ tā gāo de duō. 我比他高得多。 I am much taller than he.

To state equal degree, the phrase to be inserted is **gēn** + *obj.* + **yíyàng** 一样: same as object or as... as object. e.g.

Wǒ gēn tā yíyàng gāo. 我跟他一样高。 I am as tall as he.

Wǒ yǒu tā nème gāo. 我有他那么高。 I am as tall as he.

To state superlative degree, use the superlative adverb **zuì** 最 **dǐng** 顶 in front of the stative verb, e.g.

Wǒ zuì gāo. 我最高。 I am the tallest.

7. Verb 1 + **-zhe** 着 + Verb 2 expressing the purpose or means of V 1:

Liú zhè chī.

留着吃。　Keep it for the purpose of eating.

Děng zhè kàn (qiáo).

等着看（瞧）。　Wait and see.

Shuō zhè wán.

说着玩。　Say it for fun.

Zǒu zhè qiáo.

走着瞧。　Let's walk and see (what happens).

8. **duō** 多 **shǎo** 少 + Verb + numeral + classifier + Noun: In all these examples, the quantity is not precise.

Shǎo xǐ yí gè wǎn.

少洗一个碗。　To have one bowl less to wash.

Shǎo xiě jǐ gè zì.

少写几个字。　To write fewer characters.

Duō kàn jǐ běn shū.

多看几本书。　To read a few more books.

Duō rènshì jǐ gè rén.

多认识几个人。　Get to know more people.

Duō zuò hǎo shì.

多做好事。　Do more good deeds.

9. More examples of the disposal form **bǎ** 把:
   (See Note 3 above)

   Bǎ zhèi yīfu ná qù xǐ.

   把这衣服拿去洗。

   Take these clothes to wash.

   Bǎ zhèi wénzhāng ná qù gǎi.

   把这文章拿去改。

   Take this essay to correct.

   Bǎ zhèi běn shū ná lái kàn.

   把这本书拿来看。

   Take this book to read.

   Bǎ wèntí tíchūlái tǎolùn.

   把问题提出来讨论。

   Bring up these questions for discussion.

   Bǎ zhèi xiē liú xià lái wǎnshàng chī.

   把这些留下来晚上吃。

   Leave these things for supper to-night.

   Bǎ guǒjiàng, huángyóu tú zài kǎo miànbāo shàng.

   把果酱，黄油涂在烤面包上。

   Spread jam and butter on the toast.

   Bǎ píjiǔ fàng zài bīngxiānglǐ.

   把啤酒放在冰箱里。

   Put the beer in the fridge.

10. Verb + **wánle** 完了 ... **jiù** 就 + Verb phrase = after completing doing something then ... : (See Note 12, Lesson 4) Here le is the aspect marker meaning the completion of an action. Hence, **wán** 完 (to finish) is optional in all these examples.

    Xǐ (wán) le pénzi, jiù qù zuò gōngkè.

    洗（完）了盘子就去做功课。

— 171 —

After washing the dishes, do your homework.

Xǐ (wán) le yīfú jiù ná qù liàng.

洗（完）了衣服就拿去晾。

After washing the clothes we'll hang them up.

Zuò (wán) le zhèi yí yè jiù néng zǒu.

做（完）了这一页就能走。

After finishing this page we'll go.

11. Verb + **zài** 在 + place nouns: (See Note 3, Lesson 4, on location markers)

Gē zài zhuōr shàng.

搁在桌儿上。

Place it on the table.

Fàng zài kǒudàilǐ.

放在口袋里。

Put it in the pocket.

Là zài túshūguǎn.

落在图书馆。

Left it in the library.

Qìchē tíng zài ménkǒu.

汽车停在门口。

The car is parked outside the door.

Zìxíngchē fàng zài jiàoshǐ wàimiàn.

自行车放在教室外面。

The bicycle is left outside the classroom.

12. Superlative, degree **zuì** 最 + adjective:

zuì gāo	最高	tallest, highest
zuì pàng	最胖	fattest
zuì yǒu qián	最有钱	wealthiest
zuì hé kǒu wèr	最合口味儿	best suits one's taste
xuì yǒu rénqíng wèr	最有人情味儿	most empathic
zuì jiǎng dàoli	最讲道理	most reasonable
zuì máfan	最麻烦	most troublesome
zuì màoxiǎn	最冒险	most risky

13. Some fixed expressions with **kào** 靠: relying on or leaning against.

Kào biānr-zhàn.

靠边儿站。　　Deprived of the right to carry out one's duty.

— 172 —

Kào zhèi gè chīfàn.

靠这个吃饭。　　Make a living on this.

Tā shuōdè huà kàodezhù ma?

他说的话靠得住吗？　　Is what he says reliable?

Zhè gè rén kào bú zhù.

这个人靠不住。　　This person is unreliable.

LESSON 6

1. Directional preposition + place noun + verb = prepositional phrase of purpose:

Dào lǐbiānr zuò.

到里边儿坐。

Come inside and visit a while. (to the inside to sit)

Qù lǐtáng tīng bàogào.

去礼堂听报告。

Go to the auditorium to hear a talk.

Lái jiàoshǐ tīng kè.

来教室听课。

Come to the classroom to hear a lecture.

2. gēn 跟 + noun + verb: together with.

Gēn tā qù dǎqiú.

跟他去打球。 Play ball with him.

Gēn nǐ shuōhuà.

跟你说话。 Talk with you.

Gēn lǎoshī tǎolùn wèntí.

跟老师讨论问题。 Discuss a problem with a teacher.

Gēn wǒ qù hē chá.

跟我去喝茶。 Come to tea with me.

3. yǒu kòng 有空: to have free time.

Yǒu kòng jiùshì yǒu shíjiān.

有空就是有时间。

To have free time means to be free.

Jīntiān méiyǒu kòng, míngtiān yào kǎoshì, kǎole shì jiù yǒu kòngle.

今天没有空，明天要考试，考了试就有空了。

Today I don't have time. I have a test tomorrow. After the test I'll have time.

4. huan 换 + noun: to change, vary.

Huàn kǒu wèi.

换口味。 To vary taste = change the menu...

Huàn yīfu.

换衣服。 To change clothes.

Huàn yào.

换药。 To change the dressing.

5. The numeral one yī · · · can be omitted before a classifier without a change of meaning.

hē bēi jiǔ	喝杯酒	to have a glass of wine
chī wǎn miàn	吃碗面	to eat a bowl of noodles
chàng ge gēr	唱个歌	to sing a song

6. **shì** ... Verb + **de** 是···的 classifying the action in the past.

Wǒ shì zuótiān lái de.

我是昨天来的。 I came yesterday.

Tā shì zài Xīní chūshēng de.

他是在悉尼出生的。 He was born in Sydney.

Zhè qìchē shì Rìběn zuòde.

这汽车是日本做的。 This car was made in Japan.

7. Verb + **-qǐlai** 起来：begin to . . . V.

Shuō qǐlai róngyì zuò qǐlai nán.

说起来容易做起来难。

When you say something, it's easy; when you do it, it's difficult (Easier said than done).

Zhè huār wén qǐlai hěn xiāng.

这花闻起来很香。

When you smell this flower, it's rather fragrant.

8. Verb + **de shíhou** 的时候 (the time) when (I/you/he)

chū guó de shíhou	出国的时候	when you went overseas
huí guó de shíhou	回国的时候	when you came back
chū mén de shíhou	出门的时候	when you went out
huíjiā de shíhou	回家的时候	when I/he returned

9. Modifying noun phrase with **de** 的：

A modifier may be a word or a sentence that is converted into a phrase with the addition of **de** 的. Whereas in English the phrase usually follows the item modified, in Chinese it always precedes.

cóng wàiguó huílai de tóngxué

从外国回来的同学

students who come back from overseas (returned students)

cóng túshūguǎn jièlái de shū

从图书馆借来的书

books that are borrowed from the library

cóng fànguǎn mǎi lai de cài

从饭馆买来的菜

food bought from restaurants

cóng Mòěrběn qǐfēi de fēijī

从墨尔本起飞的飞机

planes that leave from Melbourne

LESSON 7

1. **zuìjìn** 最近 - **jìnlái** 近来:
   Jìnlái yǒu shénmè hǎo xiāoxí.
   近来有什么好消息。 Any good news lately?
   Zhèxie rìzi hěn lěng.
   这些日子很冷。 It's been very cold lately.
   Zhè jǐ tiān hěn rè.
   这几天很热。 It's been hot these last few days.

2. **yǒu** 有 + Noun + Verb marking indefiniteness in the noun:
   Yǒu rén lái kàn nǐ.
   有人来看你。
   There's someone to see you.
   Yǒu shì qǐng nǐ bāngmáng.
   有事请你帮忙。
   I have something (I need) to ask your help with.
   Yǒu huà děigēn nǐ shuō.
   有话得跟你说。
   I have something to talk to you about.

3. **gǎo** 搞: to be engaged in.
   Xuéle zhōngwén wǒ yào gǎo fǎlǜ zhuānyè.
   学了中文我要搞法律专业。
   After studying Chinese, I want to go into law.
   Xuéle zhōngwén wǒ yào gǎo kē (xué) yán (jiū).
   学了中文我要搞科(学)研(究)。
   After studying Chinese, I want to do science.
   Xuéle zhōngwén wǒ yào gǎo shèhuì diàochá.
   学了中文我要搞社会调查。
   After studying Chinese, I want to do social survey work.

4. **yè** 业: meaning some form of industry.
   Zhōngguó dè gōngyè bù fādá.
   中国的工业不发达。
   Chinese industry is not developed.
   Dì sān shìjiè dōu shì nóngyè guójiā.

第三世界都是农业国家。

The Third World consists entirely of agricultural countries.

Aòdàlìyà dè kuàngyè hé xùmùyè bǐjiǎo fādá.

澳大利亚矿业和畜牧业比较发达。

Australia's mineral and livestock industries are quite developed.

5. Emphatic adverb **dàoshì** 倒是：

Zhè dàoshì gè hǎo bànfǎ.

这倒是好办法。

This is actually a good way.

Tā dàoshì gè hǎo rén.

他倒是个好人。

He's actually a good person.

Zhè zhǒng kǎoshìfǎ dàoshì kěqǔdè.

这种考试法倒是可取的。

Actually, this way of examining is quite commendable.

6. **guówài** 国外： overseas

opposite: **guónèi** 国内： domestic

7. **xuéyuàn** 学院： institute

Lǐgōng xuéyuàn	理工学院	Institute of Technology
Nóngyè xuéyuàn	农业学院	Agricultural Institute
Tǐyù xuéyuàn	体育学院	College of Physical Culture
Wàiyǔ xuéyuàn	外语学院	Foreign Languages Institute

8. **lèisì** 类似 . . . ： Similar to

Lèisì kōuyǔdè shū hǎo dǒng, lèisì wényán dè shū nán dǒng.

类似口语的书好懂，类似文言的书难懂。

Books that are (written in a style) similar to colloquial speech
are easy to understand; books that are similar to classical
Chinese are difficult to understand.

Lèisì zhè zhǒng dè shūfǎ zhǎnlǎn bù duo.

类似这种的书法展览不多。

One doesn't see this type of calligraphy exhibition very often.

1. Common kinship terms:

	Patrilineal		Matrilineal	
	M	F	M	F
grandparents	zǔfù 祖父 (yéye) （爷爷）	zǔmǔ 祖母 (nǎinai) （奶奶）	wàizǔfù 外祖父 lǎoye （姥爷）	wàizǔmǔ 外祖母 lǎolao （姥姥）
older siblings (of parents)	dàbai 大伯 gūfu 姑父	dàniáng 大娘 gūgu 姑姑	jiùjiu 舅舅 yífu 姨父	jiùmu 舅母 yí(er) 姨（儿）
parents	bàba 爸爸 (fùqin) （父亲）			māma 妈妈 (mǔqin) （母亲）
younger siblings	shūshu 叔叔	shěr 婶儿	jiùjiu 舅舅	jiùmu 舅母
older siblings (of one's self)	gēge 哥哥	sǎosaao 嫂嫂 (sǎozi) （嫂子）	jiěfu 姐夫	jiějie 姐姐
younger siblings	dìdi 弟弟	dìxífu 弟媳妇 (dìfù) （弟妇）	mèifu 妹夫	mèimei 妹妹
spouse	zhàngfu 丈夫	qīzi 妻子		
children	érzi 儿子	nǚer 女儿		
grand children	sūnzi 孙子	sūnǚer 孙女儿		

2. Greetings according to the situation:
huí jiāle   回家了，   I'm going home.

wǒ zǒule	我走了：	I'm leaving now.
fàng xuéle	放学了：	school is out
xià bānle	下班了：	finish work for the day
shàng bānle	上班了：	going to work
chī wánle	吃完了：	I am finished eating.
màn chī	慢吃：	Enjoy the rest of your meal. (May I be excused?)

3. Contiguous numbers indicating approximation:

sì wǔ ge yuè	四、五个月	4-5 months
bā jiǔ nián	八、九年	8-9 years
bā jiǔ ge niántóu	八、九个年头	8-9 years
liǎng sān ge zhōng tóu	两三个钟头	2-3 hours
sān wǔ ge rén	三五个人	3-5 people
shí jǐ ge (shí lái ge)	十几个（十来个）	10 or more
yì bǎi duō rén	一百多人	a hundred or more people
yì qiān duō rén	一千多人	a thousand or more people

4. Conjunction jiù 就: conjoins sequentially related clauses.

Cái xuéle sì gè yuè, jiù shuōdé zhèmò hǎo le.

才学了四个月，就说得这么好了。

You've only studied for four months, yet you speak so well.

Tiān hǎo jiù kàndé hěn yuǎn.

天好就看得很远。

When the weather is fine, one can see quite a distance.

5. Indefinite yī 一 omitted from object of a verb phrase indicates 'a', 'any', 'some' etc. (See Note 5, Lesson 6)

Tiào ge wǔ 跳个舞 Give us a dance.

Jiǎng ge gùshì 讲个故事 Tell us a story.

Tǎolùn(yí)jiàn shì 讨论（一）件事 Discuss certain matters.

Jiěshì gè wèntí 解释个问题 Explain a problem.

6. gāi 该： should be ... now.

Yǐjīng qī diǎnlè, gāi zuòfàn le.

已经七点了，该做饭了。

It's already 7 p.m.; (I) should do the cooking now.

Tiān hēilè, gāi huíjiāle.

天黑了，该回家了。

It's already dark;(I) should be getting home now.

Míngtiān yào kǎoshì, gāi fùxí gōngkèlè.

明天要考试，该复习功课了。

(I've) got an exam tomorrow; (I) should review (my) notes.

7. **zǎo diǎnr** ... 早点儿：

Zǎo diǎnr shuì.

早点儿睡

Go to bed early.

Zǎo diǎnr qǐ lái.

早点儿起来。

Get up early.

Zǎo diǎnr zuòwán gōngke, kéyǐ zǎo diǎnr xiūxi.

早点儿做完功课，可以早点儿休息。

If (you) finish (your) homework early, (you) can go to bed early.

8. **xiān ... zai,** 先…再： after ... then ....

Xuélè xiàndài wén zài xué gǔwén.

学了现代文再学古文。

Study modern Chinese before studying classical Chinese.

Xiān xué shuōhuà zài xué xiě zì.

先学说话，再学写字。

Learn to speak before (you) learn to write.

9. **(jiu) yào** （就）要： will be ... soon.

(Jiù) yào xià yǔ le.

（就）要下雨了。 It's going to rain soon.

(Jiù) yào fàng jià le.

（就）要放假了。 It'll be holidays soon.

10. **háiděi** 还得： Besides ... one still, must ....

Lǎoshī zài kèwài háiděi fúdǎo xuésheng.

老师在课外还得辅导学生。

Teachers have to tutor students outside class.

Xuésheng zài kèwài háiděi bèishū liànzì.

学生在课外还得背书练字。

Students have to memorize the text and practise writing the characters outside class time.

11. **jìrán ... jiù ...,** 既然…就…： If (or, since) ... then ....

Tā jìrán shēngbìng, jiù děi xiūxi.

他既然生病，就得休息。

If he's sick, then he should take a rest.

Jìrán xià yǔ, jiù gǎi tiān zài qù ba.

既然下雨，就改天再去吧。

If it's raining, then we'll go another day. (Since it's raining, we'll go another day.)

12. **yǐqián** 以前: until now; **yǐhòu** 以后: from now on:

Yǐqián làngfèi le hěn duō shíjian.

以前浪费了很多时间。

Until now a lot of time has been wasted.

Yǐhoù yào hǎo hǎor yònggùng.

以后要好好儿用功。

From now on, I'll make a better effort.

LESSON 9

1. Preposition + Noun + Verb: (See Note 1, Lesson 6)
   shàng cài chǎng mǎi cài
   上菜场买菜　　going to the market to buy vegetables
   shàng fànguǎn chī fàn
   上饭馆吃饭　　eating out at a restaurant
   shàng fēijīchǎng jiē péngyou
   上飞机场接朋友　　meeting a friend at the airport

2. guo 过 .. aspect marker indicating past experience. (See Note 1, Lesson 1)
   Wǒmen méi xuéguo zhèxie zì.
   我们没学过这些字。
   We haven't learned these characters.
   Tā hái méi qùguò xī ào.
   我还没去过西澳。
   He hasn't been to Western Australia yet.
   Tā hái méi chīguo hóngshāo ròu.
   他还没吃过红烧肉。
   He hasn't eaten 'Red-cooked' pork before.

3. Contrast **lóushàng** (Noun)楼上 with **shànglóu** (Verb)上楼:
   Lóushàng shì bàngōngshì, lóuxià shì huìkèshì
   楼上是办公室，楼下是会客室。
   There's an office upstairs and a reception lounge downstairs.
   Shànglóu de shíhou màn, xiàlóu de shíhou kuài.
   上楼的时候慢，下楼的时候快。
   Going upstairs is slow, but coming down is fast.

4. **dào** 倒：Emphatic adverb, meaning on the contrary or contrary to what was known.
   Tā dào shì ge hǎorén.
   他倒是个好人。
   He actually is a good person.
   Zhèr de tiānqi dào hěn hǎo.
   这儿的天气倒很好。
   The weather is actually fine here.

5. **shénmè + noun + dōu + verb . . .** 什么 … 都 All inclusive, totality, any . . . all, every . . . :

Tā è le, shénme dōngxi dōu chī.

他饿了，什么东西都吃。

When he's hungry, he eats anything.

Tā hěn yònggōng, shénmò shíhòu dōu zài túshūguǎn.

他很用功，什么时候都在图书馆。

He works very hard; he's in the library all the time.

Tā zài zhè dìfang zuìjiǔ, shénmerén tā dōu rènshi.

他在这地方最久，什么人他都认识。

He has been here the longest; he knows everybody.

6. **shǒuxù** 手续: procedures.

Chūguó shǒuxù bù róngyì bàn.

出国手续不容易办。

Procedures for leaving the country are complicated.

Shàngdàxué de shǒuxù yǐjīng bànle.

上大学的手续已经办了。

Procedures for going to the university have been completed.

7. Variations on the fixed expression **chàbuduō** 差不多: more or less the same.

Zhècì kǎoshì gēn shàngcì chàbuduō.

这次考试跟上次差不多。

This time the examination was more or less like last time.

Báitiān gēn wǎnshàng de wēndù chàhěnduō.

白天跟晚上的温度差很多。

There's a big difference between the temperature during the day and during the evening.

Nǐ shuō de nàme liúlì, wǒ bǐ nǐ chà de yuǎn.

你说得那么流利，我比你差得远。

You're so fluent, I can't match you.

8. **fēnkāi** 分开: divide separately.

Chī xīcān shì yìrén yífèn fēnkāi chīde.

吃西餐是一人一份分开吃的。

When eating western meals, each person has his own portion.

Tāmen liǎng ge rén fēnkāi zhùle.

他们俩个人分开住了。

Those two are living separately now.

Tāmen hěn yàohǎo, fēn bù kāi.

他们很要好，分不开。

They're inseparable.

9. **zhao** 照， according to:

Zhàozhe zhè fāngfǎ zuò bú huì cuò de.

照着这方法做不会错的。

Follow the instructions and you can't be wrong.

Zhào jīngyàn bànshì.

照经验办事。

Act according to experience.

Zhào gāo ǎi páiduì.

照高矮排队。

Queue up according to height.

10. Verb + **qilai** 起来：begin to ... (See Note 7, Lesson 6)

Tā kàn qǐlai xiàng ge yǎn yuán.

他看起来像个演员。

He looks as if he's an actor.

Tiān (yí) rè qǐlai jiù chī bú xià fàn le.

天（一）热起来就吃不下饭了。

When it gets hot, one can't eat.

LESSON 10

1. More examples of preposition **dào** + **qù** + verb 到…去：
   Dào xuěshān qù huáxuě.
   到雪山去滑雪。
   To go skiing in the Snowy Mountains.
   Dào càichǎng qù mǎicài.
   到菜场去买菜。
   To go to market to buy food.
   Dào Běijīng qù xué pǔtōnghuà.
   到北京去学普通话。
   To go to Beijing to learn Standard Chinese.

2. **céng**, 层 .. Classifier for a layer, extended to mean a storey, a floor.
   Zhè fángzi yǒu hǎo jǐ céng.
   这座房子有好几层。　　This house has several stories.

3. Modifying noun phrase introduced by **de** 的：(See Note 9, Lesson 6)
   Wǒ gēn nǐ shuō guò de nèi ge rén.
   我跟你说过的那个人。　　The person that I told you about.
   Zuótiān jiǎng de kèwén.
   昨天讲的课文。　　The lesson that was discussed yesterday.
   Xīní lái de tóngxué.
   悉尼来的同学。　　The students who came from Sydney.

4. Some notes about **Lǐ Shízhēn** （李时珍）：
   Lǐ Shízhēn shì míngcháo shíhòu de yīshēng.
   李时珍是明朝时候的医生。
   Li Shizhen was a doctor of the Ming Dynasty.
   Tā shēng zài yī wǔ yī bā nián, sǐ zài yī wǔ jiǔ sān nián.
   他生在一五一八年，死在一五九三年。
   He was born in 1518, (and) died in 1593.
   Tā bǎ zhōngyào fēn chéng zhíwù, dòngwù hé kuàngwù sān dà lèi.
   他把中药分成植物、动物和矿物三大类。
   He divided Chinese medicines into 3 major categories—plants, animals and minerals.

Zhíwù yòu fēn chéng hǎo jǐ dà lèi.

植物又分成好几大类。

Plants are further divided into several phyla.

Dōu zhào zhíwù shēngzhǎng huánjìng lái fēnde.

都照植物生长环境来分的。

They are all grouped according to the environment in which the
plants grow.

5. Contrast "**gěi** 给 passive construction": Object + **gěi** 给 +
   subject + verb + complement, with the "**bǎ** 把 construction"
   which topicalises the object and details how the act was perform-
   ed: Subject + **bǎ** + object + verb + complement.

Indicative	*Passive* **gěi** 给	*Disposal* **bǎ** 把
Tā dǎ pò le bēizi.	**Bēizi gěi tā dǎ pòle.**	**Tā bǎ bēizi dǎ pòle.**
他打破了杯子。	杯子给他打破了。	他把杯子打破了。
He broke the cup.	The cup was broken by him.	He broke the cup.
Tā kāizǒule qìchē.	**Qìchē gěi tā kāi zǒule.**	**Tā bǎ qìchē kāi zǒule.**
他开走了汽车。	汽车给他开走了。	他把汽车开走了。
He drove the car away.	The car was driven away by him.	He drove the car away.
Gǒu yǎole xiǎojī.	**Xiǎojī gěi gǒu yǎole.**	**Gǒu bǎ xiǎojī yǎole.**
狗咬了小鸡。	小鸡给狗咬了。	狗把小鸡咬了。
The dog bit the chicken.	The chicken was bitten by the dog.	The dog bit the chicken.

LESSON 11

1. **ba** 把 + object + verb indirect object: (See note on disposal **ba** + object construction, Note 3, Lesson 5)

   Bǎ dōngxi ná gěi tā.

   把东西拿给他。　　Take this thing and give it to him.

   Bǎ dōngxi jiāo gěi tā.

   把东西交给他。　　Hand this thing to him.

   Bǎ dōngxi chuán gěi tā.

   把东西传给他。　　Pass this thing on to him.

   Bǎ dōngxi dì gěi tā.

   把东西递给他。　　Hand over this to him.

2. Topic of the sentence is object of the verb:

   Shū jiè chūqù le.

   书借出去了。　　The book was loaned out.

   Shū jiè zǒu le.

   书借走了。　　The book was checked out.

   Shū jiè dào le.

   书借到了。　　The book has been borrowed.

   Shū jiè zháo le.

   书借着了。　　The book was borrowed.

   Shū jiè wán le.

   书借完了。　　The books have all been borrowed.

3. Non-restrictive noun phrases-**yǒu** 有 + Verb + **de** 的 (N)- means "There are . . ."

   Yǒu huì zhōngwén de (rén).

   有会中文的（人）。

   There are people who know Chinese.

   Yǒu chī shèng de (cài).

   有吃剩的（菜）。

   There's food that is left over.

   Yǒu chuān guò de (yīfú).

   有穿过的（衣服）。

   There are clothes that have already been worn.

4. **tiánbiǎo** 填表: to fill in a from.

Zhèi ge biǎo wǒ bú huì tián.

这个表我不会填。

I don't know how to fill in this form.

Hěn duō shíjiān dōu huā zài tiánbiǎo shang.

很多时间都花在填表上。

Much time is used in filling out forms.

5. Verb +yi xia 一下 = verb reduplicated, tentativeness, "just," "a while":

dēngjì yí xià	登记一下	(stop for a moment) to register
tǎolùn yí xià	讨论一下	to discuss for a while
shāngliáng yí xià.	商量一下	to talk it over
xiūxì yí xià	休息一下	to rest a while

With monosyllabic verb-object compounds, **yíxià** .... is inserted in between:

tiào yíxià wǔ	跳一下舞	dance a while
shuì yíxià jiào	睡一下觉	take a nap
kàn yíxià shū	看一下书	read for a while
dǎ yíxià qiú	打一下球	to play (ball) a while

6. Noun + verb +**zài** 在 +place noun, indicating state of being, extistence:

Míngzì xiě zài kǎpiàn shang.

名字写在卡片上。 The name was written on the card.

Huàer guà zài qiáng shang.

画儿挂在墙上。 The picture was hung on the wall.

Yǎnyuán zhàn zài wǔtái shang.

演员站在舞台上。 The performer was standing on the stage.

LESSON 12

1. **bú jiù** 不就 Confirmational questions or tag questions:
   Zhè bú jiùshi nǐ yào mǎi de máobǐ ma?
   这不就是你要买的毛笔吗？
   Isn't this the kind of brush you want to buy?
   Zhè bú jiùshi wǒmen kànguo de nèi ge diànyǐn ma?
   这不就是我们看过的那个电影吗？
   Isn't this the movie we have already seen?
   Zhè bú jiùshi yǒumíng de Xīní gējùyuàn ma?
   这不就是有名的悉尼歌剧院吗？
   Isn't this the famous Sydney Opera House?

2. Sucessive actions where the first action is indicated by adverb
   xiān 先 "first" and/or aspect marker **le** 了 completed action, and
   the second action is indicated by **zài** 再.
   Xiān 先 V1 **le** 了 **zài** 再 V2:
   Xiān kàn le zài shuō
   先看了再说。
   Let's look first before we talk. (about the decision)
   Xiān zuò le shíyàn zài xiě bàogào.
   先做了试验再写报告。
   Carry out the experiment before writing the report.
   Xiān xué shuō zài xué xiě róngyì xiē.
   先学说再学写容易些。
   Learning to talk first and then to write is easier.

3. **(Hái) děi** 还得: It is not enough to ...but also have to ....
   Zhōngwén xué huì le háiděi cháng yòng, bùrán jiù wàng le.
   中文学会了还得常用，不然就忘了。
   After you have learned Chinese you have to use it often, otherwise
   you will forget it.
   **Tīng, shuō, dú, xiě hái bú gòu, háiděi zhīdào zài shénme qíngkuàng
   děi zěnme yòng.**
   听说读写还不够，还得知道在什么情况得怎么用。
   Listening, speaking, reading and writing are not enough; you
   still have to know how to use it in context.

4. **cóng ... dào** 从 … 到: Seeking information about distance,

— 190 —

cost and travel time.

Cóng zhèr dào huǒchēzhàn yǒu duō yuǎn?

从这儿到火车站有多远?

How far is the station from here?

Cóng zhèr dào huǒchēzhàn děi duōshǎo qián?

从这儿到火车站得多少钱?

How much does it cost to go from here to the station?

Cóng zhèr dào huǒchēzhàn děi zǒu duō jiǔ?

从这儿到火车站得走多久?

How long does it take to go from here to the station?

5. **lián** 连: including, together with.

   Lián tā yígòng wǔ ge rén.

   连他一共五个人。

   Including him, there are five persons altogether.

6. Substantiative predicates:

   Yí ge zì liǎng máo qián. .

   一个字两毛钱。   One word (costs) twenty cents.

   Er shí ge zì sì kuài qián.

   二十个字四块钱。   20 words (costs) four dollars.

   Er shí bā ge zì yí gòng wǔ kuài liù máo qián.

   二十八个字一共五块六毛钱。

   28 words (costs) $5.60 altogether.

7. Emphatic argument, with **lián ... dōu** 连...都:
even..., not to mention...

   lián xì dōu néng yǎn, shuōhuà hái chéng wèntí ma?

   （连）戏都能演，说话还成问题吗?

   (S)he acts well; how could (s)he have any problem with speaking?

   Lián jiǔ dōu bùnéng hē, zěnme néng xǐhuan jiǔhuì ne?

   （连）酒都不能喝，怎么能喜欢酒会呢?

   He can't even drink wine; how can he talk about enjoying cocktail parties?

   Lián zhōngwén dōu kàn bù dǒng, zěnmo néng zuò yánjiū gōngzuò ne?

   连中文都看不懂，怎么能作研究工作呢?

   (She) can't even read Chinese; how can (she) do research work?

LESSON 13

1. The subject of the topic-comment sentence is not necessarily the agent of the action.

Xìn yào jì hángkōng de.
信要寄航空的。
The letter is to be sent by airmail.

Diànbào yào dǎ pǔtōng de.
电报要打普通的。
The telegram is to be sent at ordinary rate.

2. a) Dative construction (i.e. with verbs that take indirect objects) and benefactive construction (i.e. doing something on behalf of someone else or for the benefit of . . .). Dative and benefactive constructions share the same structure on the surface, verb + object + **gei** 给 + indirect object:

Xiě (fēng) xìn gěi tā.
写封信给他。
Write him a letter.
=
Gěi tā xiě (fēng) xìn.
给他写封信。
Write a letter to him.

Dǎ (gè) diànhuà gěi tā.
打个电话给他。
Give him a call.
=
Gěi tā dǎ (gè) diànhuà.
给他打个电话。
Make a telephone call to him.
(. . . on his behalf.)

Huà (zhāng) huàr gěi tā.
画张画儿给他。
Draw a picture to give him.
=
Gěi tā huà (zhāng) huàr.
给他画张画儿。
Draw a picture for him.

b) However, the benefactives can be changed to verb + indirect object + **de** + object without affecting the meaning:

Wǒ gěi (wǒ tì; wǒ wèi) 我给（我替；我为）+ :

tā xiū chē
他修车
repair the car for him
=
xiū tā de chē
修他的车
repair his car

tā zhī máoyī
他织毛衣
knit a woollen sweater for him
=
zhī tā de máoyī
织他的毛衣
knit his woollen sweater

— 192 —

tā dǎsǎo wūzi

他打扫屋子　　　　　　　　＝

clean up the room

gěi 给 **(tì** 替—**wèi** 为)

gěi tā bāng máng

给他帮忙　　　　　　　　　＝

help him

c)　Passives:

Jī gěi gǒu yǎo le.

鸡给狗咬了。　　　　　　　＝

The hen was bitten by the dog.

Fángzi gěi chāi le.

房子给拆了。　　　　　　　＝

The house was pulled down.

Xìn gěi tuì huílái le.

信给退回来了。

The letter was returned.

dǎsǎo tā de wūzi

打扫他的屋子

clean up his room

bāng tā de máng

帮他的忙

help him out

Jī bèi gǒu yǎo le.

鸡被狗咬了。

The hen was bitten by the dog.

Fángzi bèi chāile.

房子被拆了。

The house was pulled down.

Xìn bèi tuì huílái le.

信被退回来了。

The letter was returned.

— 193 —

LESSON 14

1. **zhǎnlǎn** 展览：exibit.

   Wǒmén zuótiān qù zhǎnlǎnguǎn kàn le xiàndài huàr zhǎnlǎn.

   我们昨天去展览馆看了现代画展览。

   Yesterday we went to the gallery to see an exhibition of modern paintings.

   Tīngshuō zuìjìn zài niǔyuē jǔxíng de yícì Bìjiāsuǒ (Picasso) zhǎnlǎnhuì yòng lè sān bǎi wàn kuài qián (měijīn).

   听说最近在纽约举行的一次毕加索展览会用了三百万块钱（美金）。

   I heard that the Picasso Exhibition that was held in New York recently cost 3 million dollars (US).

2. More on indefiniteness with **yǒu** 有..

   Lǐbiār yǒu hěnduō yóupiào.

   里边有很多邮票。

   There are many stamps inside.

   Shūshang yǒu xué bù wán de hànzì.

   书上有学不完的汉字。

   There are more than enough characters in the book to learn.

   Jiālǐ yǒu duōshao rén?

   家里有多少人。

   How many people are there at home?

3. **yǎn** 演：show, perform.

   Zhè diànyǐngyuàn chángcháng yǎn wàiguó piānzi.

   这电影院常常演外国片子。

   This cinema often shows foreign films.

   Zhè jùyuàn yě yǎn jīngjù yě yǎn dìfāngxì.

   这剧院演京剧也演地方戏。

   The playhouse puts on both Beijing opera and local opera.

4. **cónglái...méi** 从来 ... **méi** 没：never.

   Cónglái méi jiànguo zhèyàng de rén!

   从来没见过这样的人！

   I have never seen this sort of person!

   Cónglái méi xiǎngguo zhè wèntí.

从来没想过这问题。

I have never thought of this question.

Wǒ cónglái bù xǐhuan kàn diànyǐng.

我从来不喜欢看电影。

I have never liked seeing films.

5. **bié** 别 = **bù** 不 + **yào** 要：

Yǒu huà hǎoshuō, xiān bié dòng shǒu.

有话好说，先别动手。

Let's talk it over calmly. Don't use your fist.

Mǎshàng jiù yào chīfàn le xiān bié chī diǎnxīn.

马上就要吃饭了，先别吃点心。

We'll soon be having a meal. Don't eat snacks yet.

LESSON 15

1. **shuang** 双, here used to mean "even" (number) but more commonly occurring in the context of **yìshuāng** 一双 measure word:

   yìshuāng kuàizi 一双筷子 a pair of chopsticks
   yìshuāng xié 一双鞋 a pair of shoes
   yìshuāng shǒu 一双手 a pair of hands

   Notice the following are in the singular:

   yífù yǎnjìng 一付眼镜 a pair of glasses
   yìtiáo kùzi 一条裤子 a pair of trousers
   yìbǎ jiǎndāo 一把剪刀 a pair of scissors

2. **bù** 不 + Stative verb + **bù** 不 + opposites:

   bú kuài bú màn 不快不慢 neither fast nor slow
   bù zǎo bù wǎn 不早不晚 neither early nor late
   bù gāo bù ǎi 不高不矮 neither tall nor short (human)

3. Approximate estimation is expressed by adding **Shàngxià** 上下.. **Zuǒyòu** 左右 to the number:

   Aòdàlìyà rénkǒu yǒu yìqiān wǔbǎi wàn shàng xià (zuǒyòu).
   澳大利亚人口有一千五百万上下（左右）。
   Australia has a population of about 15 million people.

   Míngtiān jiǔdiǎn zuǒyòu wǒ lái kān nǐ.
   明天九点左右我来看你。
   I'll come and see you round nine tomorrow.

   Dàgài yì qiān shàng xià bà.
   大概* 一千上下* 吧。
   About 1 thousand.

   Chàbùduō yí wàn zuǒyòu.
   差不多* 一万左右* 。
   Approximately 10 thousand.

4. More examples of topic + comment:

   Dēng kāi lè (Dēng liàng lè)
   灯开了（灯亮了） The light is on.

Dàgài and shàng xià (also chàbùduō and zuǒyòu) in the last sentences are only for oral expression. In written Chinese, we just write dàgài yì qiān or yì qiān shāng xià. Double estimates (dàgài and shàng xià) are rarely used together.

Dēng guān le (Dēng hēi le)

灯关了（灯黑了） The light is switched off.

5. **jiā** 加 : add, additional

Zài sùshè , guònián guòjié jiù jiā cài.

在宿舍过年过节就加菜。

In the dormitory, one gets additional dishes at new year and on holidays.

Xiànzài gōngzuò máng, jīngcháng děi jiā bān, bú guò wǒmén kěyǐ ná jiā bān fèi.

现在工作忙，经常得加班；不过我们可以拿加班费。

It is really busy at work now; we have to work extra hours but we can get overtime pay.

Zhè dōngxi shì jīngguo huàxué jiāgōng de.

这东西是经过化学加工的。

This has undergone chemical processing.

Tā zài yí ge shípǐn jiāgōng chǎng gōngzuò.

他在一个食品加工厂工作。

He works at a food processing factory.

jiā piā(n)r	加片	extra feature
jiā qián	加钱	add more money
jiā jià	加价	to raise the price
jiā yóu	加油	to refuel; to hurry up

LESSON 16

1. Emphatic negative **bìng** 并 +negative:

   Zhè gè rén bìng búxiàng rénjiā shuō de nème huài.

   这个人并不象人家说得那么坏。

   This person is not as bad as people say he is.

   Zuótiān bìng méi xiàyǔ.

   昨天并没下雨。

   It did not rain yesterday.

   Zhōngwén bìng bú xiàng xiǎngxiàng dè nème nán.

   中文并不象想象的那么难。

   Chinese is really not as hard as one imagines.

2. Verb + **le bàntiān cái/hái** (⋯了半天才/还 It took a long time before/and still) + Verb phrase:

   Wǒ gēn tā shuō le bàntiān huà hái bù zhīdào tā jiào shénme míngzi.

   我跟他说了半天话还不知道他叫什么名字。

   I talked to him for a long time and still don't know what his name is.

   Tā xiǎng le bàntiān cái xiǎng qǐlai zhège zì shì zěnme xiě de.

   他想了半天才想起来这个字是怎么写的。

   He thought for a long time before he could figure out how to write this character.

3. **mòmíngqímiào** 莫名其妙： Colloquial fixed expression of classical origin.

   Nèi gè rén zhēn mòmíngqímiào, zhèyàng yě bú shì nàyàng yě bú shì.

   那个人真莫名其妙；这样也不是，那样也不是。

   I cannot figure that person out. Nothing pleases him.

   Zhè diànyǐng bǎ tā kàn de mòmíngqímiào.

   这电影把他看得莫名其妙。

   The movie left him confused.

4. **dào** 倒... contrary to expectations: (See Note 5, Lesson 7)

   Tā bāng le ni nème duō máng, nǐ dào zhèyàng duì tā!

   他（她）帮了你那么多忙，你倒这样对他（她）！

He/she has helped you so much and you actually treat him/ her like that!

Zhōngwénshū wǒ kàn bù dǒng, búguò, zhōngguó huà wǒ dào néng tīng dǒng.

中文书我看不懂，不过中国话我倒能听懂。

I cannot read written Chinese but I can understand spoken Chinese.

(I cannot read Chinese but I can understand spoken Chinese.)

5. **qǐxiān...hòulái** 起先…后来 at first... later:

qǐxiān wǒ búhuì chá zìdiǎn hòulái xuéhuì le.

起先我不会查字典，后来学会了。

At first I didn't know how to look up things in the dictionary, but I learned later on.

Wǒ qǐxiān yǐwéi zhè shì hěn jiǎndān, hòulái cái zhīdao bìng bú nèmè jiǎndān.

我起先以为这事很简单，后来才知道并不那么简单。

At first I thought this matter was simple, but later on I realized it wasn't so simple.

6. All-inclusive noun phrase indicator **suǒ** 所， N + Suǒ 所 + V:

Nà shūshang suǒ jiǎng de lǐlùn wǒ dōu bù dǒng.

那书上所讲的理论我都不懂。

I don't understand any of the theories that were discussed in the book.

Huìshang suǒ tǎolùn de dōushi lìshǐ wèntí.

会上所讨论的都是历史问题。

What they discussed at the meeting were all historical problems.

7. **xiàng ... side (shìde)** 象…似的 It seems, it's like:

Tā zhěngtiān xiàng (shì) zài zuòmèng shìde.

他整天象（是）在做梦似的。

He seems to live in a dream world all the time.

Zhè rén xiàng shi zài nǎr jiàn guò shìde.

这人象是在哪儿见过似的。

It seems that I have seen this person somewhere.

8. Verbalizer - **huà** 化 - ize, - ization:

Zhōngguó xiàndàihuà 中国现代化。 China's modernization
rénshēng xìjùhuà 人生戏剧化。 dramatization of life
yīnyuè dàzhònghuà 音乐大众化。 popularization of music

— 199 —

9. **duō** 多 +Verb:

Duō tīng shǎo shuō.

多听少说。

Listen more and talk less.

Duō liànxí liànxí.

多练习练习。

Practise some more.

Duō xiě jǐ biàn jiù shú le.

多写几遍就熟了。

Write it a few more times and you'll get used to it.

10. **kěxī** 可惜: It is a pity.

Kěxī tā bù néng lái.

可惜他不能来。　　What a pity he can't come.

Kěxī wǒ kàn bù dǒng rìwén

可惜我看不懂日文。　　It is a pity I don't read Japanese.

LESSON 17

1. Definiteness and indefiniteness are marked by the order of the noun in the sentence; i.e., definite nouns occur first in the sentence and indefinite last or after the verb **yǒu** 有：

   Diànhuà zài nǎr?   **Nǎr yǒu diànhuà?**
   电话在哪儿？   哪儿有电话？
   Where is the telephone?   Is there a telephone?

   Gǒu zài huāyuán lǐ.   **Huāyuán lǐ yǒu gǒu.**
   狗在花园里。   花园里有狗。
   The dog is in the garden. There is a dog in the garden.

2. Explanatory or descriptive construction **shì** ...**de**是…的：

   Zhè huà shì zěnme shuō de?
   这话是怎么说的？ How do you say this? (What does it mean?)

   Zhè cài shì zěnme zuò de?
   这菜是怎么做的？ How do you cook this dish?

   Máobǐ shì zěnme yòng de?
   毛笔是怎么用的？ How do you use this brush?

3. Verbal subjects **děi** 得： have to, must.

   Chī zhōngguó fàn děi yòng kuàizi.
   吃中国饭得用筷子。
   One must use chopsticks to eat a Chinese meal.

   Yào shēnghuó jiù děi gōngzuò.
   要生活就得工作。
   In order to live, one must work.

   Dǎ diànbào děi qù diànbàojú.
   打电报得去电报局。
   To send a telegram, one must go to the Telegraph Office.

4. **Xiān**...**zài**...先...再： first...then.

   Xiān shuō zài xiě.
   先说再写。 Say it first and then write it.

   Xiān mǎi piào zài jìnqu.
   先买票再进去。 Buy your ticket before entering.

5. Reduplicating the verb to show politeness: (See Note 11, Les-

son 1 and Note 5, Lesson 3)

(Qǐng) nǐ kànkan zhè jùzi xiě de duì bú duì.

（请）你看看这句子写得对不对？

Would you see if this sentence is written correctly?

Jìnlai zuòzuo.

进来坐坐。

Come in and sit a spell.

Děng yi děng jiù lái le.

等一等就来了。

Wait a while, and (we)'ll be there.

LESSON 18

1. More examples on benefactives gěi 给 + indirect object + verb + direct object

   Lǎoshī gěi wǒ jiěshì wèntí.

   老师给我解释问题。

   The teacher explained the problem to me.

   Wǒ gěi tā mǎi dōngxi.

   我给他买东西。

   I bought some things for him. (I shopped for him)

   Shīfu gěi tā zuò cài.

   师傅给他做菜。

   The chef prepared some dishes for him.

2. **Yǒu shì** 有事: have business, be busy or occupied.

   Wǒ yǒu shì jiù qù zhǎo ta.

   我有事就去找他。

   I go to him whenever I need help.

   Tā méi shì jiù lái liáo tiānr.

   他没事就来聊天。

   When he doesn't have anything to do he comes over for a chat.

   Wǒ zuótiān yǒu shì bù néng lái.

   我昨天有事不能来。

   I was busy yesterday so I was not able to come.

3. Restrictive noun phrases with the noun omitted. (See Note 9, Lesson 6)

   Tīng de dǒng zhōngwén dè hé tīng bù dǒng zhōngwén dè dōu qù kàn nàge diànyǐng le.

   听得懂中文的和听不懂中文的都去看那个电影了。

   Those who understand Chinese and those who don't understand Chinese all went to see the movie.

   Zuótiān cái xué dè jīn tiān zěnmò néng bèi?

   昨天才学的今天怎么能背？

   How can we recite what was only learned yesterday?

LESSON 19

1. Verb + Result compound: (See Note 2, Lesson 5 and Note 2, Lesson 23)

Wǒ zuó tian kàn dào yīng guó nǔ-huáng le.

我昨天看到英国女皇了。

I saw the Queen of England yesterday.

Nǐ dè xìn wǒ shōu dào lè.

你的信我收到了。

I have received your letter.

Nèi běn shū hěn duō rén yào kàn, lǎo jiè bù dào.

那本书很多人要看，老借不到。

So many people want to read that book that it is never available.

2. Time expressions:

jīnnián	今年	this year
míngnián	明年	next year
qùnián	去年	last year
qiánnián	前年	the year before last
hòunián	后年	the year after next
jīntiān	今天	today
míngtiān	明天	tomorrow
zuótiān	昨天	yesterday
qiántiān	前天	the day before yesterday
hòutiān	后天	the day after tomorrow
zhè ge yuè	这个月	this month
xià ge yuè	下个月	next month
shàng ge yuè	上个月	last month
shàng shàng ge yuè	上上个月	the month before last
xià xià ge yuè	下下个月	the month after next
zhè ge xīngqī	这个星期	this week
xià ge xīngqī	下个星期	next week
shàng ge xīngqī	上个星期	last week
shàng shàng ge xīngqī	上上个星期	the week before last
xià xià ge xīngqī	下下个星期	the week after next
zhè ge zhōngtou	这个钟头	this hour

xià ge zhōngtou	下个钟头	next hour
shàng ge zhōngtou	上个钟头	last hour (past hour)
liǎng ge zhōngtóu qián	两个钟头前	two hours before
liǎng ge zhōngtóu hòu	两个钟头后	two hours after
liǎng diǎn yí kè	两点一刻	15 past 2 2.15
sān diǎn bàn	三点半	half past 3 3.30
sì diǎn sān kè	四点三刻	15 to 5 4.45

3. Emphatic use of hái 还: need to, still.

Zánmen zènme shú, hái yòng kèqì?

咱们这么熟，还用客气？

We know each other so well; must we be so formal?

Zhè wèntí suīrán jiǎndān, hái děi xiǎng yì xiǎng.

这问题虽然简单，还得想一想。

Although this matter may be simple, it still needs more thought.

LESSON 20

1. Adjectives or adverbs, like verbs, may be reduplicated to show liveliness. The repeated word is changed into the first tone (if not already in the first tone) with the addition of the retroflexed-r ending and optional **de** 地：

   dā → **dàdār de**   大 → 大大儿地   good and big
   màn → **mànmār de**   慢 → 慢慢儿地   good and slow

   A disyllabic adjective ab is changed into aabb:

   lǎoshi → **lǎolǎoshíshi de**   老实 → 老老实实地   good and honest
   rènzhēn → **rènrènzhēnzhēn de**   认真 → 认认真真地   earnest

2. **tí** 提：to bring up.

   Zhè wèntí tā yǐjīng zài huìshang tí chū lái tǎolùn lè.
   这问题他已经在会上提出来讨论了。
   He has already brought up the question for discussion at the meeting.

   Qǐng nǐ tí yìjiàn.
   请你提意见。
   Please make some comments.

   Yàzhōu xuéshēng hěn shǎo zài jiàoshì lǐ tí wèntí.
   亚洲学生很少在教室里提问题。
   Asian students rarely ask questions in class.

3. **chūchāi**, 出差：

   Chūchāi jiù shì yīnwéi gōng shì dào bié dè dì fāng qù dè yìsi.
   出差就是因为公事到别的地方去的意思。
   Chuchai means going to another place for business.

   Yǒu dè rén chūchāi dè shíhòu jiù shì chūqù wár.
   有的人出差的时候就是出去玩儿。
   Some people go on business just to get away for pleasure.

4. **lùguò** 路过：to pass by.

   Cóng dàxué dào shì zhōngxīn yào lùguò yīnyuè xuéyuàn.
   从大学到市中心要路过音乐学院。
   To go from the university to the city centre, you must pass by the conservatory.

Tā lùguò wǒ jiā dè shíhòu cháng jìnlái liáotiānr.

他路过我家的时候常进来聊天儿。

When he passes by my house, he often comes in for a chat.

5. **huàn** 换: to change.

   Cóng wàiguó dào Aòzhōu dè fēijī zǒng děi zài Xīní huò Mòérběn huàn fēijī cái néng dào Kǎnpéilā.

   从外国到澳洲的飞机总得在悉尼或墨尔本换飞机才能到堪培拉。

   International flights to Australia all involve changing in Sydney or Melbourne in order to get to Canberra.

   Huàn chē shíjiān chángde hěn, yǒu zhídá chē zuì hǎo.

   换车的时间长得很，有直达车最好。

   It takes a long time to change trains. It would be best if there was a direct train.

6. **yàobù** 要不 = **yào bú rán** 要不然 = otherwise: This expression is often used to negate a previous statement and suggest an alternative.

   bùle 不了 = **bú yào le** 不要了 = No, I don't.

7. **qí** 骑: to ride on a vehicle or an animal.

   Qíchē duì shēntǐ hǎo, qí mǎ ne?

   骑车对身体好，骑马呢？

   Riding bicycles is good for one's health, how about riding horses?

   Nǐ huì qí dānlúnchē ma?

   你会骑单轮车吗？

   Can you ride a monocycle?

8. **yìqǐ** 一起: together.

   Wǒmén tiāntiān yìqǐ xuéxí, yìqǐ zuò gōngkè.

   我们天天一起学习，一起做功课。

   Everyday we study and do our homework together.

   Yǒu shì dàjiā yìqǐ zuò róngyì dé duò.

   有事大家一起做容易得多。

   It's much easier to work out problems together.

9. **jiào** 叫: to call.

   Zhèr dè chūzhū qìchē bù néng zài lùshàng jiào de.

   这儿的出租汽车不能在路上叫的。

   One cannot hail a taxi in the streets here.

   Jiào sānlúnchē qù yě xíng.

   叫三轮车去也行。

   It would be alright to go by (calling a) pedi-cab.

LESSON 21

1. **tíng** 停： stop, park.
   Wǒ de biǎo tíngle, bù zǒule.
   我的表停了，不走了。
   My watch has stopped; it's not working anymore.
   Dàmén kǒu bù néng tíng chē.
   大门口不能停车。
   One cannot park outside the main gate.

2. **fúwùyuán** 服务员： (service) assistant clerk, waiter, waitress.
   Zhè ge fúwùyuán de tàidù bù hǎo, nǐ wèn yíjù, tā cái huídá yí jù.
   这个服务员的态度不好；你问一句，他才回答一句。
   The clerk's attitude is not very good; he answers questions only
      when he is asked.

3. **guǎngbō** 广播： (radio) broadcast.
   Nǐ měitiān dōu shōu tīng něi ge guǎngbō diàntái?
   你每天都收听哪个广播电台？
   Which radio stations do you listen to everyday?
   Dāng guǎngbō yuán de fāyīn děi hěn biāo zhǔn.
   当广播员的发音得很标准。
   The pronunciation of radio announcers must be up to standard.

4. **zhùyì** 注意： take notice of, attention
   Nǐ zhùyì kàn zhè ge zì gēn něi ge zì de xiě fǎ bù yí yàng.
   你注意看这个字跟那个字的写法不一样。
   Pay attention the way this character is written differently from
      that character.
   Tā shēntǐ bu tài hǎo duō zhùyì yí xià.
   他身体不太好，多注意一下。
   His health is not good; take good care of him.

LESSON 22

1. ràng 让: to allow, cause.

   Bú ràng tā yǒu chuàng xīn dè jīhuì.

   不让他有创新的机会。

   Don't give him the opportunity to innovate.

   Ràng nǐ děng le zènme jiǔ, zhēn bàoqiàn.

   让你等了这么久，真抱歉。

   I apologise for making you wait so long.

2. yì...jiù... 一···就··· as soon as.

   Láohǔ yì pū guòlai Wǔsōng jiù shǎn kāi le.

   老虎一扑过来，武松就闪开了。

   As soon as the tiger pounced on him, Wusong dodged swiftly to one side.

   Tiān yì dǎléi, jiù xiàyǔ le.

   天一打雷，就下雨了。

   As soon as it thunders, it starts to rain.

3. zìjǐ 自己: self.

   Tā zìjǐ dǎ zìjǐ de zuǐba.

   他自己打自己的嘴巴。

   He contradicts himself. (He hits his own mouth.)

   Zìjǐ zuò de shì, zìjǐ yào fùzé.

   自己做的事，自己要负责。

   One must be responsible for one's own actions.

4. chángchang 尝尝: to try by tasting.

   Zhèi diǎnxīn hái búcuò nǐ chángchang kàn.

   这点心还不错，你尝尝看。

   These appetizers are quite good; try a piece.

   Qǐng chángchang zhèi zhǒng xīn cǎi de chá.

   请尝尝这种新采的茶。

   Please try this newly picked tea.

5. dài 带 directional complement lái, 来: towards speaker or qù,
   去: away from speaker. (See Note 4, Lesson 5)

   Wǒ chángcháng dài háizi qù tīng yīnyuè.

   我常常带孩子去听音乐。

I often take the children to concerts.

Tā cóng Hángzhōu dài lái le yì xiē xīn chá.

他从杭州带来了一些新茶。

He's brought some new tea from Hangzhou.

6. Intensifier **guài** 怪：

Rénjia shuō tā yǒu nǚpéngyǒu, tā guài bù hǎo yìsi de.

人家说他有女朋友，他怪不好意思的。

When people mention that he has a girl friend, he becomes embarrassed.

Zhè shì shénme liúxíng yīnyuè, guài nántīng de.

这是什么流行音乐？怪难听的。

What kind of popular music is this? It sounds awful!

LESSON 23

1. **ānpái** 安排: plan, program, arrangements.

Zìjǐ děi zhǔdòng xiē, bú yào zǒng děng lǐngdǎo ānpái.

自己得主动些，不要总等领导安排。

One must take more initiative and not always wait for the leader's orders.

Zhè yàng ānpái fēicháng línghuó.

这样安排非常灵活。

Arranging it this way is rather flexible.

Ānpái de tài sǐ rénjiā jiù huì gǎn dào bèidòng.

安排得太死，人家就会感到被动。

If the plan is too rigid, people will feel put upon.

2. Verb + result **dào** 到: up to; to reach; the goal that one sets out to.

Zhè běn xiǎoshuō wǒ yǐjīng kàn dào sānbǎi yè le.

这本小说我已经看到三百页了。

I have read to page 300 in this novel.

Lǎoshī jiǎng kè jiǎng dào yíbàn, jiù wèn wǒmen wèntí.

老师讲课讲到一半，就问我们问题。

Halfway through the lecture, the teacher asked us questions.

Wǒ mǎi dào piào le.

我买到票了。

I have bought the tickets.

3. Rhetorical or confirmative questions **búshì**:不是

Nǐ bú shì shuōguo rénmín yào yǒu yánlùn hé chūbǎn de zìyóu ma?

你不是说过人民要有言论和出版的自由吗？

Didn't you say that people should have freedom of speech and publication?

Nǐ bú shì jīntian wǎnshang yào lái ma?

你不是今天晚上要来吗？

Aren't you coming tonight?

4. **lǎolao** 姥姥: kinship term for maternal grandmother used as direct term of address. (See Note 1, Lesson 8)

Běifāng rén guǎn mǔqīn de māma jiào lǎolao, guǎn fùqīn de māma jiào nǎinai.

北方人管母亲的妈妈叫姥姥，管父亲的妈妈叫奶奶。

Northerners call their mother's mother *laolao*, and their father's mother, *nainai*.

5. Intensifier **kě** 可：

Zhè huí tā kě cāi zhòng le.

这回他可猜中了。

He guessed it right this time. (in contrast to previous attempts)

Zhè xiàzi kě máfán le.

这下子可麻烦了。

This time we're really in trouble. (We were just lucky before.)

6. **dàniáng** 大娘：direct term of address for an older woman.

Niánjì bǐjiào dà de nǚde jiào dàniáng.

年纪比较大的女的叫大娘。

Older women are called daniang.

Dàniáng de nánren jiù jiào dàbai.

大娘的男人就叫大伯。

The husband is called dabai.

Nánfāng rén guǎn dànián jiào bómǔ, guǎn dàbai jiào bófù huò bóbo.

南方人管大娘叫伯母，管大伯叫伯父或伯伯。

Southerners call daniang *bomu* and dabai *bofu* or *bobo*.

7. **lǎorénjia** 老人家：old folks, also a respectful term of address to refer to elderly people. As such it is used together with pronouns **nǐ lǎorénjia** 你老人家 and **tā lǎorénjia** 他老人家.

Lǎorénjia shi zūnjìng de chēnghu.

老人家是尊敬的称呼。

Laorenjia is a respectful term of address.

Tā lǎorénjia shēntǐ hái hǎo ba?

他老人家身体还好吧？

Is he in good health?

8. More examples of predicates used as topics:

Cānjiā yánjiǎng bǐsài hǎo.

参加演讲比赛好。

It's good to participate in speech contests.

Xiǎoháir méiyou rén zhàogù zěnme xíng.

小孩儿没有人照顾怎么行。

It's not right to leave children unattended.

Shuōhuà suàn huà.

说话算话。

A promise is a promise.

Shuō zǒu jiù zǒu.

说走就走。

When she says go she means go.

LESSON 24

1. Contiguous numbers used to indicate approximates:
   (See Note 3, Lesson 15)

   Yì nián zhǐ shàng bā jiǔge yuè de kè.

   一年只上八、九个月的课

   Classes last only 8 or 9 months a year.

   Àozhōu rénkǒu yǒu yì qiān sìwǔ bǎi wàn.

   澳洲人口有一千四五百万

   The population of Australia is between 14 and 15 million.

   Yì liǎngge fángjiān róngyì zhǎo.

   一两个房间容易找。

   It's easy to find one or two rooms.

2. **dēngjì** 登记： to register.

   Zhèr shǒuxù hěn duō, yì huǐr yào dēngjì zhèige, yì huǐr yào dēngjì nàge.

   这儿手续很多，一会儿要登记这个，一会儿要登记那个。

   There's a lot of red tape here; you must put your name on this and that.

3. **lìngwài** 另外： extra, not included.

   Tāmen chúle báitiān de gōngzuò, wǎnshang lìngwài háiděi zuò línggōng.

   他们除了白天的工作，晚上另外还得做零工。

   Besides daytime work, they have to do part-time work at night.

   Lìngwài háiyǒu yíjiànshì děi gēn nǐ shāngliang.

   另外还有一件事得跟你商量。

   I have another matter to discuss with you.

4. **zhè jiù zǒu** 这就走＝**zhè huǐr jiù zǒu** 这会儿就走。

   Wǒ zhè jiù zǒu.

   我这就走。　　I'll be going now.

   Wǒ zhè jiù gàosong tā.

   我这就告诉他。　　I'll tell him right away.

LESSON 25

1. Acknowledging presence according to the situation as a form of greeting:

   Nǐ huíláile (a). 你回来了（啊）。 You're back.

   Nǐ xǐtóule (a). 你洗头了（啊）。 You've washed your hair.

   Nǐ yě mǎicài. 你也买菜。 You're shopping too.

2. More verbal measures:

   Shàngxīngqi dào xuěshān qù wár le yítàng.

   上星期到雪山去玩了一趟

   Last week I made a holiday trip to the Snowy Mountains.

   Zhè gùshi wǒmen tīng-guo jǐ biàn le.

   这故事我们听过几遍了。

   We have heard this story several times.

   Jīnnián wǒ xiǎokǎo kǎole sāncì dōu jígé.

   今年我小考考了三次都及格。

   I have passed all 3 tests this year.

   Tā kǎoshàngle yánjiūyuàn quánjiā jiù dào fànguǎn qù dà chī le yí dùn.

   他考上了研究院，全家就到饭馆去大吃了一顿。

   After he passed the entrance exam for graduate school, the whole family went to have a feast in a restaurant.

3. **xièr** 馅儿 = **xiàn** + **r,** 馅 + 儿： filling for buns, rolls, dumplings.

   Jiǎozi xièr yǒu hūnde yě yǒu sùde.

   饺子馅儿有荤的有素的。

   There are dumpling fillings with meat and without meat.

   Hūnde yì bān dōu shì zhūròu hé báicài.

   荤的一般都是猪肉和白菜。

   The ones with meat are generally with pork and cabbage.

   Sùde suíbiàn shénme cài dōu kěyǐ, yǒu shíhou yě fàng fěnsī hé jīdàn.

   素的随便什么菜都可以，有时候也放粉丝和鸡蛋。

   As for vegetarian *jiaozi*, any kind of vegetable will do. Sometimes one can add bean threads and eggs.

4. **huó (miàn)** 和（面）： to mix (dough).

— 215 —

Zuò miàntiáor de miàn bù néng huòde tài ruǎn.

做面条儿的面不能和得太软。

The dough for noodles must not be too soft.

Zhè xièr bǐng de miàn huò de tài yìng le.

这馅儿饼的面和得太硬了。

The dough for meat pancakes is too dry.

5. **Fèi (shi)** 费（事）： give or take a lot of trouble.

Zhè shì zuò qǐlai hěn fèi gōngfu.

这事做起来很费功夫。

This work is very time consuming.

Fèishì de shì yào dàhuǒr yìqǐ lái gàn.

费事的事要大伙儿一起来干。

Everyone must chip in to do work that requires a lot of effort.

6. **Féngnián guòjié** 逢年过节 = **Guònián guòjié** 过年过节： celebrating New Year and other festivals.

Guònián guòjié de shíhou jiājiā dōu hěn rènào.

过年过节的时候家家都很热闹。

During the New Year and on festivals every family is buzzing with activity.

7. **V + zhe** 着 **+ diǎnr** 点儿： used as a polite command or reminder.

Guò mǎlù kànzhe diǎnr.

过马路看着点儿。

Be careful (watch out) when you cross the street.

Zhè shìer ni jìzhe diǎnr.

这事儿你记着点儿。

Don't forget about this matter.

PRONUNCIATION PRACTICE

(Adapted from *Mandarin Primer*)

Listen to the tape, repeating each sound or group of sounds at the appropriate pause. Beginning Chinese speakers should complete each exercise several times. Finally, as a self-test of your ability to relate each sound to its orthography, use the tape for dictation practice. Write each sound you hear in *pinyin*, including tone marks, keeping the book closed. Then check your work against the text.

Exercise A: TONES

1. Single tones

ā	á	ǎ	à
mā	má	mǎ	mà
yī	yí	yǐ	yì
fēi	féi	fěi	fèi
tāng	táng	tǎng	tàng

2. Tones in combination

a) tā tīng   he listens
   tā lái   he comes
   tā mǎi   he buys
   tā mài   he sells

b) méi tīng   did not listen
   méi lái   did not come
   méi mǎi   did not buy
   méi mài   did not sell

c) nǐ tīng   you listen
   nǐ lái   you come
   nǐ mǎi   you buy
   nǐ mài   you sell

d) **yào tīng**	wants to listen
yào lái	wants to come
yào mǎi	wants to buy
yáo mài	wants to sell

3. Neutral tones

a) **tīng le**	has heard
lái le	has come
mǎi le	has bought
mài le	has sold
b) **sān ge**	three
yí ge	one, a
wǔ ge	five
liù ge	six
c) **fēi de**	that which flies
pá de	that which crawls
pǎo de	that which runs
tiào de	that which jumps

Exercise B: DIFFICULT SOUNDS

1. Consonants:
   a) Unaspirated and aspirated voiceless initials
   English consonant in "by" contrasted with Chinese consonants, as in "spy" (pinyin *b*) and "pie" (pinyin *p*)

bèng	to hop
pèng	to collide
lǎo bèng	always hopping
lǎo pèng	always colliding

   English consonant in "deem" contrasted with Chinese consonants, as in "steam" (pinyin *d*) and "team" (pinyin *t*)

duì	correct
tuì	retreat
duì le	that's correct
tuì le	have retreated

   English consonant in "gate" as contrasted with Chinese consonants, as in "skate" (pinyin *g*) and "Kate" (pinyin *k*)

gàn	to do
kàn	to look
gàn wán le	to finish doing
kàn wán le	to finish looking

   English consonant in "soothe" contrasted with Chinese consonants, as in "zoo" (pinyin *z*) and "tsunami" (pinyin *c*)

zuì	drunk
cuì	crisp
zuì le ba	Drunk, I suppose?
cuì le ba	Is it crisp?

   b) Retroflexes *zh, ch,* and *sh*

zhū bù lái	The pig doesn't come.
chū bù lái	cannot come out
shū bù lái	The book hasn't arrived.

   (Note that lips are not spread with the above finals)

zhàng	zhàng le	to have swollen
chàng	chàng le	to have sung
shàng	shàng le	to have taken up
zhǎo	yào zhǎo	to want to look for
chǎo	yào chǎo	to want to fry
shǎo	yào shǎo	to want (something) to be less

(Note that lips are spread with the above finals)

c) The retroflex *r* is not trilled and is shorter than in English.

rù	rù kǒu	entrance (doorway)

(Note that lips are not spread)

rén	yí ge rén	one person

(Note that lips are spread)

d) To pronounce initials *ji, qi,* and *xi,* think of the English "jeep," "cheese," and "she," but spread your lips.

jiāng	wǒ méi jiāng	I have no ginger.
qiāng	wǒ méi qiāng	I have no gun.
xiāng	wǒ méi xiāng	I have no incense.

e) Review of some difficult initials.

zhòu	yīfu zhòu le	The clothes are wrinkled.
jiù	yīfu jiù le	The clothes are old.
chàng	tā chàng le	She has sung.
qiāng	tā qiāng le	He choked on something.
shǎo	tài shǎo le	too few; too little
xiǎo	tài xiǎo le	too small
ròu	tā mǎi ròu le	he bought meat

2. Vowels

a) In *zì, cì,* and *sì,* the vowel *i* is like a vocalized *z.*

zì	zì	word
cì	cì	thorn
sì	sì	four

— 220 —

b) In *zhì*, *chì*, and *shì*, the vowel *i* is like a prolonged *r*, with lips spread.

rì	rì	day
zhì	zhì	heal
chì	chì	wing
shì	shì	affair

c) Practice the combination *uō*.

guǒ	fruit
duō shuō	talk much
wǒ shuō	I say

d) Distinguish between *ie* and *ue*.

xiē xie	rest a bit
xiè xie	Thank you.
dà yuē	approximately
dà xué	university

e) Practice nazalized retroflex vowels.

míngr	tomorrow
dà shēngr	loudly
yàngr	form
chóngr	insect

f) A final *n* should not be linked to a following vowel or semi-vowel.

sān èr	three two
wén yán	literary language
zhēn hǎo	very nice

Exercise C: REVIEW OF INDIVIDUAL SOUNDS AND TONES

Read the following in all four tones:

di	di	di	di
yi	yi	yi	yi
du	du	du	du
wu	wu	wu	wu
yu	yu	yu	yu
diu	diu	diu	diu
zha	zha	zha	zha
jia	jia	jia	jia
zhua	zhua	zhua	zhua
e	e	e	e
ye	ye	ye	ye
yue	yue	yue	yue
wo	wo	wo	wo
xi	xi	xi	xi
shi	shi	shi	shi
chen	chen	chen	chen
qin	qin	qin	qin
chun	chun	chun	chun
qun	qun	qun	qun
shu	shu	shu	shu
xiu	xiu	xiu	xiu
ai	ai	ai	ai
wai	wai	wai	wai
leng	leng	leng	leng
ling	ling	ling	ling
ge	ge	ge	ge
guo	guo	guo	guo
ni	ni	ni	ni
nu	nu	nu	nu
niu	niu	niu	niu
a	a	a	a

ya	ya	ya	ya
ang	ang	ang	ang
yang	yang	yang	yang
wa	wa	wa	wa
wang	wang	wang	wang
ren	ren	ren	ren
run	run	run	run
shei	shei	shei	shei
shui	shui	shui	shui
hai	hai	hai	hai
an	an	an	an
eng	eng	eng	eng
huai	huai	huai	huai
ying	ying	ying	ying
san	san	san	san
zhong	zhong	zhong	zhong
jiong	jiong	jiong	jiong
suan	suan	suan	suan
dei	dei	dei	dei
dui	dui	dui	dui
mao	mao	mao	mao
miao	miao	miao	miao
ou	ou	ou	ou
you	you	you	you
le	le	le	le
luo	luo	luo	luo
lie	lie	lie	lie
lue	lue	lue	lue
yan	yan	yan	yan
yuan	yuan	yuan	yuan
wan	wan	wan	wan
jin	jin	jin	jin
zhen	zhen	zhen	zhen
zhun	zhun	zhun	zhun
jun	jun	jun	jun

Tones	Pinyin	Meaning
— — —	sanxian tang	three-flavor soup
— — ／	shuo yingwen	speak English
— — ✓	duo he shui	drink a lot of water
— — ＼	ta shuo hua	he talks
— —	kai deng ba	Turn on the light.
— ／ —	dongnan feng	southeast wind
— ／ ／	san nian ji	third-year class
— ／ ✓	xianren zhang	cactus
— ／ ＼	xihong shi	tomato
— —	he cha de	one who drinks tea
— ✓ —	ta ye shuo	she also says
— ✓ ／	ta lao lai	he always comes
— — ✓	sanyan jingr	Three-hole Well (street name)
— ✓ ＼	wo mai cai	I buy vegetables.
— ✓	zhen gan ji	really grateful
— ＼ —	jidangao	sponge cake
— ＼ ／	ta yao cha	He wants tea.
— ＼ ✓	shu tai xiao	The book is too small.
— ＼ ＼	shuang guahao	to register with return receipt
— ＼	ta e le	He's hungry.
— —	ga zhi wo	armpit
— ／	shuo de lai	congenial
— ✓	ting bu dong	cannot understand
— ＼	zhong guo hua	Chinese language
—	fei lai le	has flown here
／ — —	shei xian shuo	Who speaks first?
／ — ／	Luguo Qiao	Marco Polo Bridge
／ — ✓	wu hua guo	fig
／ — ＼	hong shao rou	pork stewed in soy sauce
／ —	lai chi ba	Come and eat.
／ ／ —	Mei Lanfang	name of famous Chinese opera performer
／ ／ ／	hai mei lai	has not yet come
／ ／ ✓	wanquan dong	to understand completely

´ ´ `	**xunyang jian**	cruiser
´ ´	**hua chuan ba**	Let's go boating.
´ ˇ –	**huo huo shan**	active volcano
´ ˇ ´	**cong nar lai**	From where?
´ ´ ˇ	**Qin Huang Dao**	place name
´ ˇ `	**Baita Si**	White Pagoda Temple
´ ˇ	**lai wan le**	has come late
´ ` –	**chang xingfengr**	long envelope
´ ` ´	**youdian ju**	post office
´ ` ˇ	**shi er dian**	twelve o'clock
´ ` `	**wu xian dian**	radio
´ `	**mei kan jian**	have not seen
´ –	**nan de duo**	much more difficult
´ ´	**yi ge ren**	one person
´ ˇ	**shei de bi**	Whose writing brush?
´ `	**xue bu hui**	unable to learn
´	**Wang Xiansheng**	Mr. Wang
ˇ – –	**lao chou yen**	always smoking (tobacco)
ˇ – ´	**hao xinwen**	good news
ˇ – ˇ	**fangsha chang**	cotton factory
ˇ – `	**huoche jan**	train station
ˇ –	**mai xigua**	buy watermelon
ˇ ´ –	**Beimen Jie**	North Gate Street
ˇ ´ ´	**liang tiao yu**	two fish
ˇ ´ ˇ	**ni mei dong**	You didn't understand.
ˇ ´ `	**wo mei kongr**	I have no time.
ˇ ´	**haojile**	That's wonderful.
´ ˇ –	**you ji zhang**	How many sheets are there?
´ ˇ ´	**lao xiang lai**	always wanting to come
´ ´ ˇ	**wo ye you**	I also have (something).
´ ˇ `	**ni ye hui**	You also can (do something).
´ ˇ	**lao Li ne**	How about Li?
ˇ ` –	**gankuai shuo**	Hurry up and say it.
ˇ ` ´	**ni wen shei**	Who are you asking?
ˇ ` ˇ	**bi tai ruan**	The writing brush is too soft.

✓ ＼ ＼	**da dian hua**	to phone
✓ ＼	**zou zhei bianr**	Go this way.
✓ —	**zou bu kai**	cannot get away
✓ ／	**liang ge ren**	two people
✓ ✓	**xiang de hen**	desire very much
✓ ＼	**sang zi da**	loud-voiced
✓	**yizi ne**	Where's a chair?
＼ — —	**Jiu Jinshan**	San Francisco
＼ — ／	**Daxi Yang**	Pacific Ocean
＼ — ✓	**Dizhong Hai**	Mediterranean Sea
＼ — ＼	**buzhidao**	I don't know.
＼ —	**di san ge**	third
＼ ／ —	**zixing che**	bicycle
＼ ✓ ／	**zhu yangfang**	live in a foreign-style house
＼ ／ ✓	**diantai hao**	The radio station is good.
＼ ／ ＼	**douyar cai**	beansprouts
＼ ／	**xing Wang de**	one named Wang
＼ ✓ —	**liu zhan deng**	six lamps
＼ ✓ ／	**tiaoshui tai**	diving platform
＼ ／ ✓	**zizhi lour**	wastebasket
＼ ✓ ＼	**wangyuan jing**	telescope
＼ ✓	**zai nar ne**	Where is it?
＼ ＼ —	**zuo qiche**	to ride in an automobile
＼ ＼ ／	**da wenti**	great problem
＼ ＼ ✓	**kan dianyingr**	see a movie
＼ ＼ ＼	**dagai hui**	probably would
＼ ＼	**xianzai ne**	Right now?
＼ —	**dao le jia**	arrived home
＼ ／	**jiu shi nan**	It's just that it's hard.
＼ ✓	**dou funaor**	soft bean curd
＼ ＼	**kan de jian**	able to see
＼	**dui le ba**	That's correct, isn't it?

INDEX